A GOLFER'S LITTLE DEVOTIONAL BOOK

Published by Worthy Inspired, a division of Worthy Media, Inc.,
134 Franklin Road, Suite 200, Brentwood, Tennessee 37027.

Scripture references marked KJV are from the Holy Bible, King James Version

Scripture references marked NKJV are from the Holy Bible, New King James Version. Copyright © 1982 by Thomas Nelson, Inc. Used by permission.

Scripture references marked NCV are from the New Century Version®. Copyright © 1987, 1988, 1991 by Word Publishing, a division of Thomas Nelson, Inc. All rights reserved. Used by permission.

Scripture references marked HCSB are from the Holman Christian Standard Bible™ Copyright © 1999, 2000, 2001 by Holman Bible Publishers. Used by permission.

Scripture references marked NIV are from the Holy Bible, New International Version®. Copyright © 1973, 1978, 1984 International Bible Society. Used by permission of Zondervan. All rights reserved.

Scripture references marked NLT are from the Holy Bible. New Living Translation. Copyright © 1996 Tyndale Charitable Trust. Used by permission of Tyndale House Publishers.

Scripture references marked NASB are from the New American Standard Bible®. Copyright © 1960, 1962, 1963, 1968, 1971, 1972, 1973, 1975, 1977, 1995 by The Lockman Foundation. Used by permission.

Scripture references marked MSG are from the Message. Copyright © 1993, 1994, 1995, 1996, 2000, 2001, 2002. Used by permission of NavPress Publishing Group.

Cover Design by Kim Russell / Wahoo Designs
Page Layout by Bart Dawson

Printed in the United States of America

1 2 3 4 5—RRD—18 17 16 15 14

A GOLFER'S LITTLE DEVOTIONAL BOOK

WORTHY
Inspired

No other game combines the wonder
of nature with the discipline of sport
in such carefully planned ways.
A great golf course both frees
and challenges a golfer's mind.

—

Tom Watson

INTRODUCTION

In your hands, you hold a collection of devotions containing ideas that apply to the game of golf and, more importantly, to the game of life. On these pages, you'll find timeless truths from God's Holy Word along with timely insights from some of golf's greatest legends.

On the golf course, some players win; some don't; life goes on; and, in time, those numbers on the scorecards are forgotten. But, the game of life is different: it has eternal implications.

So, as you read ideas on these pages and weave them into the fabric of your daily life, pay special attention to God's guidance, to God's commandments, and to God's promises. Golf wisdom can help you craft a winning strategy for life on the links, but God's wisdom doesn't stop there . . . and neither should you.

CELEBRATING GOLF AND LIFE

This is the day that the Lord has made. Let us rejoice and be glad today!

Psalm 118:24 NCV

Why do we love the game of golf? It is a sport that combines the best that nature and man have to offer. Golf offers opportunities for relaxation, companionship, and accomplishment. Its rules are almost always self-enforced, making it a game of character and sportsmanship. The challenge of competition is present on every shot because the golfer competes not only with others, but also with himself. Who can deny the joy of a well-hit drive or the satisfaction of sinking a testy putt?

The 118th Psalm reminds us that today, like every other day, is a cause for celebration. Today is a nonrenewable resource—once it's gone, it's gone forever. Our responsibility, of course, is to use this day in the service of God's will and according to His commandments.

Today, whether you're on the golf course or not, treasure the time that God has given you. Give Him the glory and the praise and the thanksgiving that He deserves. And search for the hidden possibilities that God has placed along your path. This day is a priceless gift from God, so use it joyfully and encourage others to do likewise. After all, this is the day the Lord has made....

TODAY'S BIG IDEAS ABOUT GOLF AND LIFE

All our life is a celebration for us; we are convinced, in fact, that God is always everywhere. We sing while we work...we pray while we carry out all life's other occupations.

St. Clement of Alexandria

A round of golf should permit eighteen inspirations.

A. W. Tillinghast

A TIMELY TIP

Every day should be a cause for celebration. By celebrating the gift of life, you protect yourself from the dangers of pessimism, regret, hopelessness, and bitterness.

Rejoice in the Lord always. Again I will say, rejoice!

Philippians 4:4 NKJV

HE OFFERS PEACE

Peace I leave with you; My peace I give to you; not as the world gives do I give to you. Do not let your heart be troubled, nor let it be fearful.

John 14:27 NASB

The familiar words of John 14:27 remind us that Jesus offers us peace, not as the world gives, but as He alone gives. Have you found God's peace, or are you still rushing after the illusion of "peace and happiness" that the world promises but cannot deliver?

This day, complete with its assortment of ups and downs, is a gift from the Creator. This day will contain many blessings. This day will provide quiet moments for prayer and praise. And, this day offers yet another opportunity to welcome the Father into your heart and to share His good news with the world.

Genuine peace can be found on the golf course, or just about any other place, for that matter. Peace depends, not upon your circumstances, but upon your relationship with God. So honor Him and thank Him: It's the right thing to do—in good times and in hard times—and it's the best way to live.

TODAY'S BIG IDEAS ABOUT GOLF AND LIFE

A buoyant, positive approach to the game is as basic as a sound swing.

Tony Lema

Sometimes we get tired of the burdens of life, but we know that Jesus Christ will meet us at the end of life's journey. And, that makes all the difference.

Billy Graham

And the peace of God, which transcends all understanding, will guard your hearts and your minds in Christ Jesus.

Philippians 4:7 NIV

TODAY'S SCORE CARD

Jot Down Your Thoughts About . . .
Finding Genuine Peace

ALWAYS KEEP LEARNING

If you need wisdom—if you want to know what God wants you to do—ask him, and he will gladly tell you. He will not resent your asking.

James 1:5 NLT

The stoic philosopher Epictetus observed, "No great thing is created suddenly." And so it is with a golf swing. Proper technique may take years to achieve and a lifetime to master. That's why the serious golfer understands that his education is ongoing.

Jack Nicklaus, perhaps the greatest golfer ever to swing a club, advised, "Don't be afraid to take a lesson. I'm not." And if it's good enough for the Golden Bear, it's good enough for the rest of us.

Today is your classroom: what will you learn? Will you use today's experiences as tools for personal growth, or will you ignore the lessons that life and God are trying to teach you? Will you carefully study God's Word, and will you apply His teachings to the experiences of everyday life? The events of today have much to teach. You have much to learn. May you live—and learn—accordingly.

TODAY'S BIG IDEAS ABOUT GOLF AND LIFE

Always keep learning. It keeps you young.

Patty Berg

The wonderful thing about God's schoolroom is that we get to grade our own papers. You see, He doesn't test us so He can learn how well we're doing. He tests us so we can discover how well we're doing.

Charles Swindoll

The wise man gives proper appreciation in his life to his past. He learns to sift the sawdust of heritage in order to find the nuggets that make the current moment have any meaning.

Grady Nutt

✕ A TIMELY TIP ✕

No matter how long you've been playing the game of golf or the game of life, you still have lots to learn. So it's always the right time to learn something new.

Remember what you are taught, and listen carefully to words of knowledge.

Proverbs 23:12 NCV

15

GOD HAS A PLAN
FOR YOU

"I say this because I know what I am planning for you," says the Lord. "I have good plans for you, not plans to hurt you. I will give you hope and a good future."

Jeremiah 29:11 NCV

God has plans for your life that are far grander than you can imagine. But He won't force you to follow His will; to the contrary, He has given you free will, the ability to make choices and decisions on your own. The most important decision of your life is, of course, your commitment to accept Jesus Christ as your personal Lord and Savior. And once your eternal destiny is secured, you will undoubtedly ask yourself "What now, Lord?" If you earnestly seek God's will for your life, you will find it...in time.

Sometimes, God's plans are crystal clear, but other times, He may lead you through the wilderness before He delivers you to the Promised Land. So be patient, keep praying, and keep seeking His will for your life. When you do, you'll be amazed at the marvelous things that an all-powerful, all-knowing God can do.

GREAT IDEAS FROM GOLFING GREATS

The perfect round of golf has never been played. It's 18 holes-in-one. I almost dreamt it once, but I lipped out at 18.

Ben Hogan

The constant undying hope for improvement makes golf so exquisitely worth playing.

Bernard Darwin

In golf, while there is life, there is hope.

Sir Walter Simpson

TODAY'S SCORE CARD

Jot Down Your Thoughts About . . .
God's Plan for You and Yours

_____

_____

_____

_____

_____

_____

THE ART OF ACCEPTANCE

One thing I do, forgetting those things which are behind and reaching forward to those things which are ahead, I press toward the goal for the prize of the upward call of God in Christ Jesus.

Philippians 3:13-14 NKJV

Sometimes, we must accept life on its terms, not our own. The game of life, like the game of golf, unfolds in unpredictable ways. And sometimes, there is precious little we can do to change things.

When events transpire that are beyond our control, we have a choice: we can either learn the art of acceptance, or we can make ourselves miserable as we struggle to change the unchangeable.

We must entrust the things we cannot change to God. Once we have done so, we can prayerfully and faithfully tackle the important work that He has placed before us: doing something about the things we can change . . . and doing it sooner rather than later.

Can you summon the courage and the wisdom to accept life on its own terms? If so, you'll most certainly be rewarded for your good judgment.

IMPROVING YOUR SWING

Keep a picture of the follow-through in your head. If you get a clear picture in your mind of what you want to do, and you understand it, then your body will do it.

Marlene Floyd

Find a swing that feels comfortable and works for you, and then practice until you can groove the swing.

Nancy Lopez

I've always tried to swing at about 85 percent of my top speed. That's a pace I can control.

Sam Snead

✂ A TIMELY TIP ✂

Acceptance means learning to trust God more. Today, think of at least one aspect of your life that you've been reluctant to accept, and then prayerfully ask God to help you trust Him more by accepting the past.

Come to terms with God and be at peace; in this way good will come to you.

Job 22:21 HCSB

THE POWER OF FAITH

For whatever is born of God overcomes the world. And this is the victory that has overcome the world—our faith.

1 John 5:4 NKJV

Every life—including yours—is a series of wins and losses. Every step of the way, through every triumph and tragedy, God walks with you, ready and willing to strengthen you. So the next time you find your character being tested, whether you're on the links or not, remember to take your fears to the Giver of all good gifts. If you call upon Him, you will be comforted. Whatever your challenge, whatever your trouble, God can handle it.

When you place your faith, your trust, indeed your life in the hands of your Heavenly Father, you'll receive a lesson in character-building from the ultimate Teacher. So strengthen your faith through praise, through worship, through Bible study, and through prayer. And trust God's plans. With Him, all things are possible, and He stands ready to open a world of possibilities to you . . . if you have faith.

PERFECTING YOUR PUTTING

Maintain acceleration by not taking the putter back too far.

Al Geiberger

The putt is the payoff in golf. Unless you can putt well, the rest is merely exercise.

Sandra Haynie

There are six fundamentals of putting: grip, balance, steadiness, eyes over the line, square shoulders, and a low smooth swing.

Curtis Strange

✗ A TIMELY TIP ✗

If your faith is strong enough, you and God—working together—can move mountains.

Have faith in the LORD your God and you will be upheld.

2 Chronicles 20:20 NIV

21

BEYOND TOUGH TIMES

When you pass through the waters, I will be with you; and through the rivers, they shall not overflow you. When you walk through the fire, you shall not be burned, nor shall the flame scorch you. For I am the Lord your God, The Holy One of Israel, your Savior.

Isaiah 43:2-3 NKJV

On the links, all of us encounter occasional disappointments and setbacks: Those occasional visits from Old Man Trouble are simply a fact of life and a part of golf. The fact that we encounter adversity is not nearly so important as the way we choose to deal with it. When tough times arrive, we have a clear choice: we can begin the difficult work of tackling our troubles . . . or not. When we summon the courage to look Old Man Trouble squarely in the eye, he usually blinks. But, if we refuse to address our problems, even the smallest annoyances have a way of growing into king-sized catastrophes.

When we are troubled, or weak, or sorrowful, or angry, God is always with us. We must build our lives on the rock that cannot be shaken: we must trust in God. And then, we must get on with the hard work of tackling our problems . . . because if we don't, who will? Or should?

GREAT IDEAS FROM GOLFING GREATS

One bad shot does not make a losing score.

Gay Brewer

The worse you're performing, the harder you must work mentally and emotionally. The greatest and toughest art in golf is "playing badly well." All the true greats have been masters at it.

Jack Nicklaus

You don't have the game you played last year or last week. You only have today's game. It may be far from your best, but that's all you've got. Harden your heart and make the best of it.

Walter Hagen

TODAY'S SCORE CARD

Jot Down Your Thoughts About . . .
Overcoming Adversity

HE IS SUFFICIENT

The Lord is my rock, my fortress, and my deliverer.

Psalm 18:2 HCSB

It is easy to become overwhelmed by the demands of everyday life, but if you're a faithful follower of the One from Galilee, you need never be overwhelmed. Why? Because God's love is sufficient to meet your needs. Whatever dangers you may face, whatever heartbreaks you must endure, God is with you, and He stands ready to comfort you and to heal you.

The Psalmist writes, "Weeping may endure for a night, but joy comes in the morning" (Psalm 30:5 NKJV). But when we are suffering, the morning may seem very far away. It is not. God promises that He is "near to those who have a broken heart" (Psalm 34:18 NKJV).

If you are experiencing the intense pain of a recent loss, or if you are still mourning a loss from long ago, perhaps you are now ready to begin the next stage of your journey with God. If so, be mindful of this fact: the loving heart of God is sufficient to meet any challenge, including yours.

GREAT IDEAS FROM GOLFING GREATS

Thinking instead of acting is the number one disease in golf.

Sam Snead

Great players concentrate on cause rather than result.

Cary Middlecoff

I'm as good a player as I think I am. If you can't win in your dreams, forget it.

Calvin Peete

✕ A TIMELY TIP ✕

Whatever you need, God can provide. He is always sufficient to meet your needs.

———————————————

The LORD is my strength and song, and He has become my salvation.

Exodus 15:2 NASB

25

WISDOM ON THE LINKS . . . AND OFF

A wise man will hear and increase learning, and a man of understanding will attain wise counsel.

Proverbs 1:5 NKJV

Sometimes, amid the demands of daily life, we lose perspective. Life seems out of balance, and the pressures of everyday living seem overwhelming. What's needed is a fresh perspective, a restored sense of balance . . . and God's wisdom.

American humorist Kin Hubbard once observed, "Lots of folks confuse bad management with destiny." Often, we are tempted to blame our missed shots on bad luck, but the truth usually hits closer to home. In the words of Shakespeare, "The fault, dear Brutus, lies not in our stars, but in ourselves."

The quickest way to lower your score is to play wisely, focus your thoughts and manage your game. When you do, you'll improve your life and your handicap.

The more wisdom enters our hearts, the more we will be able to trust our hearts in difficult situations.

John Eldredge

GREAT IDEAS FROM GOLFING GREATS

Some people think they are concentrating when they're merely worrying.

Bobby Jones

You can't hit a good five-iron if you're thinking about a six-iron on your back swing.

Charles Coody

You must swing smoothly to play golf well. And you must be relaxed to swing smoothly.

Bobby Jones

A TIMELY TIP

If you'd like to become a little wiser, the place to start is with God. And His wisdom isn't very hard to find; it's right there on the pages of the Book He wrote.

_____

The fear of the Lord is the beginning of wisdom; a good understanding have all those who do His commandments. His praise endures forever.

Psalm 111:10 NKJV

27

DAY 10

WHEN TO SOLVE PROBLEMS

Therefore, get your minds ready for action, being self-disciplined, and set your hope completely on the grace to be brought to you at the revelation of Jesus Christ.

1 Peter 1:13 HCSB

Sometimes, when the challenges of the day seem overwhelming, we may spend more time worrying about our troubles than fixing them. A far better strategy, of course, is to pray as if everything depended entirely upon God and to work as if everything depended entirely upon us.

Golf, like life, is an exercise in problem-solving. The question is not whether we will encounter problems on the links; the question is how we will choose to address them.

When it comes to solving the problems of everyday living, we often know precisely what needs to be done, but we may be slow in doing it, especially if what needs to be done is difficult or uncomfortable for us. So we put off till tomorrow what should be done today. Unfortunately, most problems are not self-solving. So, it's best to face problems sooner (while they're still small) rather than later (when they're fully grown).

TODAY'S BIG IDEAS ABOUT GOLF AND LIFE

Golf is a game that is played on a five-inch course—the distance between your ears.

Bobby Jones

Golf is more in your mind than in your clubs.

Bruce Crampton

Hitting the ball isn't all there is to golf. The right mental approach can be just as important as a golfer's swing.

Gay Brewer

TODAY'S SCORE CARD

Jot Down Your Thoughts About . . .
The Most Important Thing You've Been Putting Off

THE RIGHT KIND OF ATTITUDE

God did not give us a spirit that makes us afraid but a spirit of power and love and self-control.

2 Timothy 1:7 NCV

Marcus Aurelius observed, "Man must be arched and buttressed from within, else the temple waivers to the dust." And like a good man or woman, a good golf game depends almost entirely upon inner strength.

Gary Player wrote, "There's absolutely no question that golf is a game of mind over matter." And, of course, he was right.

All too often, a bogey is simply a physical manifestation of the self-fulfilling prophesy. We become better golfers once we convince ourselves that the same may be said of birdies.

The next time you find yourself dwelling upon the negative aspects of your golf game or your life, refocus your attention on things positive. The next time you find yourself falling prey to the blight of pessimism, stop yourself and turn your thoughts around. You'll never complain your way to the top . . . so don't even try.

GREAT IDEAS FROM GOLFING GREATS

Never tell yourself you can't make a shot. Remember, we are what we think we are.

Gary Player

Golf is a matter of confidence. If you think you cannot do it, there is no chance you will.

Henry Cotton

Aptitude starts with attitude.

Greg Norman

✕ A TIMELY TIP ✕

On the golf course, as in life, a positive attitude leads to positive results. So train yourself to look for possibilities, not obstacles.

Keep your eyes focused on what is right, and look straight ahead to what is good.

Proverbs 4:25 NCV

ASK HIM

So I say to you: Ask and it will be given to you; seek and you will find.

Luke 11:9 NIV

How often do you ask God for His help and His wisdom? Occasionally? Intermittently? Whenever you experience a crisis? Hopefully not. Hopefully, you've acquired the habit of asking for God's assistance early and often. And hopefully, you have learned to seek His guidance in every aspect of your life.

The Bible promises that God will guide you if you let Him. Your job is to let Him. But sometimes, you will be tempted to do otherwise. Sometimes, you'll be tempted to go along with the crowd; other times, you'll be tempted to do things your way, not God's way. When you feel those temptations, resist them.

God has promised that when you ask for His help, He will not withhold it. So ask. Ask Him to meet the needs of your day. Ask Him to lead you, to protect you, and to correct you. And trust the answers He gives.

God stands at the door and waits. When you knock, He opens. When you ask, He answers. Your task, of course, is to seek His guidance prayerfully, confidently, and often.

IMPROVING YOUR SWING

The key to a good swing is maintaining balance.

Gary McCord

The challenge in a golf stroke is to maintain a perfect balance between firmness and relaxation in the interests of control and rhythm.

Bobby Jones

Don't press. You can hit hard without pressing.

Harry Vardon

✕ A TIMELY TIP ✕

When you ask God for His assistance, He hears your request—and in His own time, He answers.

Until now you have not asked for anything in my name. Ask and you will receive, so that your joy will be the fullest possible joy.

John 16:24 NCV

TRUST GOD'S TIMING

I waited patiently for the LORD; and He inclined to me, and heard my cry.

Psalm 40:1 NKJV

The Bible teaches us to trust God's timing in all matters, but we are sorely tempted to do otherwise, especially when times are tough. When we are beset with problems, we are understandably anxious for a quick conclusion to our hardships. We know that our problems will end some day, and we want it to end NOW. God, however, works on His own timetable, and His schedule does not always coincide with ours.

God's plans are perfect; ours most certainly are not. So we must learn to trust the Father in good times and hard times. No exceptions.

Today, as you face the uncertainties of everyday life, do your best to turn everything over to God. Whatever "it" is, He can handle it. And you can be sure that He will handle it when the time is right.

Will not the Lord's time be better than your time?

C. H. Spurgeon

GREAT IDEAS FROM GOLFING GREATS

Play the shot you've got the greatest chance of playing well.

Tommy Armour

Course management? It means you are in control of the golf course, rather than vice versa.

Patty Sheehan

Don't be ashamed to play safe.

Arnold Palmer

TODAY'S SCORE CARD

Jot Down Your Thoughts About . . .
The Wisdom of Trusting God's Timing

_____

_____

_____

_____

_____

_____

_____

KEEP PRAYING

Anyone who is having troubles should pray.

James 5:13 NCV

God is trying to get His message through . . . to you! Are you listening?

Perhaps, if you're experiencing tough times or uncertain times, you may find yourself overwhelmed by the press of everyday life. Perhaps you forget to slow yourself down long enough to talk with God. Instead of turning your thoughts and prayers to Him, you may rely upon our own resources. Instead of asking God for guidance, you may depend only upon your own limited wisdom. A far better course of action is this: simply stop what you're doing long enough to open your heart to God; then listen carefully for His directions.

Do you spend time each day with God? You should. Are you in need? Ask God to sustain you. Are you troubled? Take your worries to Him in prayer. Are you weary? Seek God's strength. In all things great and small, seek God's wisdom and His grace. He hears your prayers, and He will answer. All you must do is ask.

Prayer accomplishes more than anything else.

Bill Bright

GREAT IDEAS FROM GOLFING GREATS

I believe golf can bring you happiness.

Harvey Penick

Play golf to the hilt. Win, lose, or draw, good day or bad, you'll be happier for it, and you'll live longer.

Arnold Palmer

Keep your sense of humor. There's enough stress in the rest of your life to let bad shots ruin a game you're supposed to enjoy.

Amy Alcott

✕ A TIMELY TIP ✕

Prayer changes things and it changes you. So pray.

Whatever you ask for in prayer, believe that you have received it, and it will be yours.

Mark 11:24 NIV

YOU'RE NEVER ALONE

The LORD himself goes before you and will be with you; he will never leave you nor forsake you. Do not be afraid; do not be discouraged.

Deuteronomy 31:8 NIV

If God is everywhere, why does He sometimes seem so far away? The answer to that question, of course, has nothing to do with God and everything to do with us.

When we begin each day on our knees, in praise and worship to Him, God often seems very near indeed. But, if we ignore God's presence or—worse yet—rebel against it altogether, the world in which we live becomes a spiritual wasteland.

Are you tired, discouraged or fearful? Be comforted because God is with you. Are you confused? Listen to the quiet voice of your Heavenly Father. Are you bitter? Talk with God and seek His guidance. Are you celebrating a great victory? Thank God and praise Him. He is the Giver of all things good.

In whatever condition you find yourself, wherever you are, whether you are happy or sad, victorious or vanquished, troubled or triumphant, celebrate God's presence. And be comforted. God is not just near. He is here.

GREAT IDEAS FROM GOLFING GREATS

Do your best, one shot at a time, and then move on.
Remember that golf is just a game.

Nancy Lopez

Don't linger too long in thinking about your shots—
good or bad—but stamp the good ones into your mind
for future reference.

Greg Norman

Don't take your bad shots home with you.

Tony Lema

TODAY'S SCORE CARD

Jot Down Your Thoughts About . . .
God's Love for You and Yours

_____

_____

_____

_____

_____

ACCEPTING ADVICE

A wise man will hear and increase learning, and a man of understanding will attain wise counsel.

Proverbs 1:5 NKJV

On the golf course, advice is everywhere. Go to any practice tee and ask the first person you see for help. You'll find no shortage of tips: Keep your head down, keep your elbow in, keep your arm straight, stay loose, concentrate, bend your knees, keep your balance, have a firm grip, don't hold the club too tightly, follow through, swing hard, swing easy, and so forth.

The same is true in the game of life: advice, it seems, is everywhere.

If you find yourself caught up in a difficult situation, it's time to start searching for knowledgeable friends and mentors who can give you solid advice. Why do you need help evaluating the person in the mirror? Because you're simply too close to that person, that's why. Sometimes, you'll be tempted to give yourself straight A's when you deserve considerably lower grades. On other occasions, you'll become your own worst critic, giving yourself a string of failing marks when you deserve better. The truth, of course, is often somewhere in the middle.

Finding a wise mentor is only half the battle. It takes just as much wisdom—and sometimes more—to act upon good advice as it does to give it. So find people you can trust, listen to them carefully, and act accordingly.

GREAT IDEAS FROM GOLFING GREATS

Each player ought to have a style which is the reflection of himself, his build, his mind, his age, and his previous habits.

Sir Walter Simpson

All the vital technical parts of the swing take place in back of you, or above the head. It's terrifying to think of all the gremlins that can creep into your game. The margin for error is infinitesimal.

Roger Maltbie

 A TIMELY TIP

If you can't seem to listen to constructive criticism with an open mind, perhaps you've got a severe case of old-fashioned stubbornness. If so, ask God to soften your heart, open your ears, and enlighten your mind.

DAY 17

RESPECT YOURSELF

For you made us only a little lower than God, and you crowned us with glory and honor.

Psalm 8:5 NLT

Do you place a high value on your time and your talents? Hopefully so. After all, you are created by God, with an array of unique gifts and opportunities, all of which He wants you to use. But if you've acquired the unfortunate habit of devaluing your efforts or yourself, it's now time to revolutionize the way that you think about your career, your capabilities, your opportunities, and your future.

Nobody can build up your self-confidence if you're unwilling to believe in yourself. And the world won't give you very much respect until you decide to respect yourself first. So if you've been talking yourself down or selling yourself short, stop. Remember: If you want to enjoy real abundance—and if you want to be comfortable in your own skin—you need a healthy dose of self-respect . . . a dose that nobody can administer but you.

You are valuable just because you exist. Not because of what you do or what you have done, but simply because you are.

Max Lucado

TODAY'S BIG IDEAS ABOUT GOLF AND LIFE

Always visualize your shot.

Ken Venturi

Forget your opponents; always play against par.

Sam Snead

Always put score ahead of pride.

Ken Venturi

✕ A TIMELY TIP ✕

That quiet little voice inside your head will guide you down the right path if you listen carefully. So listen, learn, and behave accordingly. You'll feel better about yourself when you do.

You're blessed when you're content with just who you are—no more, no less. That's the moment you find yourselves proud owners of everything that can't be bought.

Matthew 5:5 MSG

THE MENTAL GAME

Those who are pure in their thinking are happy, because they will be with God.

Matthew 5:8 NCV

The French philosopher Paul Valéry could have been talking about life on the links when he observed, "We hope vaguely but dread precisely." In golf, as in life, we sometimes allow our worries to overwhelm thoughts and cloud our vision. What's needed is clearer perspective, renewed faith, and a different focus.

When we focus on the frustrations of today or the uncertainties of tomorrow, we rob ourselves of peace in the present moment. But, when we focus on God's grace, and when we trust in the ultimate wisdom of God's plans for our lives, our worries no longer tyrannize us.

Today, remember that God is infinitely greater than the challenges that you face. Remember, too, that your thoughts are profoundly powerful, so guard them accordingly.

Your thoughts are the determining factor as to whose mold you are conformed to. Control your thoughts and you control the direction of your life.

Charles Stanley

GREAT IDEAS FROM GOLFING GREATS

You don't have to hit the ball perfectly to win. You just have to manage yourself better.

Tom Watson

Many golfers can't concentrate because they're too self-conscious.

Sam Snead

A bad attitude is worse than a bad swing.

Payne Stewart

✕ A TIMELY TIP ✕

When you experience tough times (and you will), a positive attitude makes a big difference in the way you tackle your problems.

So prepare your minds for service and have self-control.

1 Peter 1:13 NCV

CONQUERING THE FRUSTRATIONS

A hot-tempered man stirs up dissention, but a patient man calms a quarrel.

Proverbs 15:18 NIV

During his heyday, Tommy Bolt's temper was infamous. Bolt could fling a club with the best of them. In fact, Jimmy Demaret proclaimed, "Tommy Bolt's putter had more air time than Lindbergh." But even the mercurial Bolt knew the value of self-control. He once admitted, "It's a game of patience." So much for air-born putters.

Publilius Syrus once observed, "Anger tortures itself." It might be added that on golf courses—or off—runaway emotions are the most dangerous hazards.

As long as you live here on earth, you will face countless opportunities to lose your temper over small, relatively insignificant events: a traffic jam, a spilled cup of coffee, an inconsiderate comment, or a missed four-foot put. When you are tempted to lose your temper over the minor inconveniences of life, don't. Turn away from anger, stress, bitterness, and regret. Turn instead to God. When you do, you'll be following His commandments and giving yourself a priceless gift . . . the gift of peace.

TODAY'S BIG IDEAS ABOUT GOLF AND LIFE

Ask yourself how many shots you would have saved if you never lost your temper, never got down on yourself, always developed a strategy before you hit, and always played within your own capabilities.

Jack Nicklaus

Anger is the noise of the soul; the unseen irritant of the heart; the relentless invader of silence.

Max Lucado

Don't become angry quickly, because getting angry is foolish.

Ecclesiastes 7:9 NCV

TODAY'S SCORE CARD

Jot Down Your Thoughts About . . .
The Rewards of Self-Control

_____

_____

_____

_____

_____

_____

COURSE MANAGEMENT

Commit your work to the LORD, and then your plans will succeed.

Proverbs 16:3 NLT

Ben Hogan said, "Management—placing the ball in the right position for the next shot—is eighty percent of winning golf." And the same thing is true in the game of life: It pays to plan.

Have you fervently asked God to help prioritize your life? If so, then you're continually inviting your Creator to become a full-fledged partner in your endeavors.

When you make God's priorities your priorities, you will receive God's abundance and His peace. When you make God a full partner in every aspect of your life, He will lead you along the proper path: His path. When you allow God to play a role in the organization of your day, He will honor you with spiritual blessings that are simply too numerous to count. So, as you plan for the day ahead, take a few quiet moments to gather your thoughts and consult your Creator. It's the best way to plan your day and your life.

TODAY'S BIG IDEAS ABOUT GOLF AND LIFE

Think ahead. Golf is a next-shot game.

Billy Casper

In God's plan, God is the standard for perfection. We don't compare ourselves to others; they are just as fouled up as we are. The goal is to be like him; anything less is inadequate.

Max Lucado

God has a plan for your life . . . do you?

Criswell Freeman

⚜ A TIMELY TIP ⚜

It isn't that complicated: If you plan your steps carefully, and if you follow your plan conscientiously, you will probably succeed. If you don't, you probably won't.

But the noble man makes noble plans, and by noble deeds he stands.

Isaiah 32:8 NIV

49

LIVE COURAGEOUSLY

He will not fear bad news; his heart is confident, trusting in the Lord. His heart is assured; he will not fear.

Psalm 112:7-8 HCSB

S am Snead, in discussing the topic of golfing courage, recalled an old Virginia adage: "The Good Lord hates a coward, but he's not real fond of a fool, either." These words seem to sum up a grand paradox of golf: Both courage and cowardice are often punished. Yet, cowardice seems to be punished more. So, it pays to be courageous.

God is with you always, listening to your thoughts and prayers, watching over your every move. If the demands of everyday life weigh down upon you, you may be tempted to ignore God's presence or—worse yet—to lose faith in His promises. But, when you quiet yourself and acknowledge His presence, God will touch your heart and restore your courage.

At this very moment, God is seeking to work in you and through you. He's asking you to live abundantly and courageously . . . and He's ready to help. So why not let Him do it . . . starting now?

GREAT IDEAS FROM GOLFING GREATS

Action before thought is the ruination of most of your shots.

Tommy Armour

If it takes you a wood to reach the green and your playing partner a five-iron, what's the difference? Make your game your own game.

Nancy Lopez

Preparing yourself for the course you're about to play is a big part of course management.

Billy Casper

✕ A TIMELY TIP ✕

If you trust God completely and without reservation, you have every reason on earth—and in heaven—to live courageously. That's precisely what you should do.

So do not fear, for I am with you; do not be dismayed, for I am your God. I will strengthen you and help you; I will uphold you with my righteous right hand.

Isaiah 41:10 NIV

51

ANXIOUS?

Be anxious for nothing, but in everything by prayer and supplication, with thanksgiving, let your requests be made known to God.

Philippians 4:6 NKJV

On the links, anxiety is the enemy. Overly anxious golfers don't win tournaments.

We live in a fast-paced, stress-inducing, anxiety-filled world that oftentimes seems to shift beneath our feet. Sometimes, trusting God is difficult, especially when we become caught up in the incessant demands of an anxious world.

When you feel stressed to the breaking point—and you will—return your thoughts to God's love and God's promises. And as you confront the challenges of golf and life, turn all of your concerns over to your Higher Power.

The same God who created the universe will comfort and guide you if you ask Him...so ask Him. Then watch in amazement as your anxieties melt into the warmth of His loving hands.

Worry and anxiety are sand in the machinery of life; faith is the oil.

E. Stanley Jones

GREAT IDEAS FROM GOLFING GREATS

Be yourself. Play within yourself. Play your own game.

Harvey Penick

Believe you can do anything, and then take a stab at it.

Nancy Lopez

The difference between ordinary players and champions is the way they think.

Patty Berg

✕ A TIMELY TIP ✕

Work hard, play hard, and pray harder. And, if you have any worries, take them to God—and leave them there.

_____

When my anxious thoughts multiply within me, Your consolations delight my soul.

Psalm 94:19 NASB

WINNING AND LOSING

Keep your eyes focused on what is right, and look straight ahead to what is good. Be careful what you do, and always do what is right. Don't turn off the road of goodness; keep away from evil paths.

Proverbs 4:25-27 NCV

The legendary football coach Knute Rockne proclaimed, "The price for victory is hard work." Rockne's words may hold true on the football field, but winning golf requires more. Cool nerves and savvy course management are also necessities.

Gene Sarazen, fresh from a win over Walter Hagen, was hospitalized for an emergency appendectomy. Commenting on his victory from the hospital bed, Sarazen confessed, "A sick appendix is not as difficult to deal with as a five-foot putt." Five-foot putts often represent the thin line between victory and defeat. For the squeamish player, those five feet can seem like five miles.

In tournament play, one player wins and the rest don't. Thankfully, the game of life is different: a single endeavor may have many winners. The price of victory is hard work, plus teamwork, plus faith, with a few other things thrown in for good measure.

GREAT IDEAS FROM GOLFING GREATS

Be brave if you lose and meek if you win.

Harvey Penick

Win graciously.

Arnold Palmer

Successful competitors want to win. Head cases want to win at all costs.

Nancy Lopez

✕ A TIMELY TIP ✕

Some people may try to convince you that winning is the most important thing. But the Bible makes it clear that doing what's right is far more important than winning a round of golf.

Take delight in the Lord, and He will give you your heart's desires.

Psalm 37:4 HCSB

55

FORGIVENESS NOW

All bitterness, anger and wrath, insult and slander must be removed from you, along with all wickedness. And be kind and compassionate to one another, forgiving one another, just as God also forgave you in Christ.

Ephesians 4:31-32 HCSB

The world holds few if any rewards for those who remain angrily focused upon the past. Still, the act of forgiveness is difficult for all but the most saintly men and women. Are you mired in the quicksand of bitterness or regret? If so, you are not only disobeying God's Word, you are also wasting your time.

Being frail, fallible, imperfect human beings, most of us are quick to anger, quick to blame, slow to forgive, and even slower to forget. Yet as Christians, we are commanded to forgive others, just as we, too, have been forgiven.

If there exists even one person—alive or dead—against whom you hold bitter feelings, it's time to forgive. Or, if you are embittered against yourself for some past mistake or shortcoming, it's finally time to forgive yourself and move on. Hatred, bitterness, and regret are not part of God's plan for your life. Forgiveness is.

TODAY'S BIG IDEAS ABOUT GOLF AND LIFE

Golf is good for the soul. You get so mad at yourself you forget to hate your enemies.

Will Rogers

Sometimes, we need a housecleaning of the heart.

Catherine Marshall

And forgive us our sins, for we ourselves also forgive everyone in debt to us. And do not bring us into temptation.

Luke 11:4 NKJV

TODAY'S SCORE CARD
Jot Down Your Thoughts About . . . The Rewards of Making Peace with Your Past

DAY 25

FINDING STRENGTH IN TURBULENT TIMES

I can do all things through Christ who strengthens me.

Philippians 4:13 NKJV

God's love and support never changes. From the cradle to the grave, God has promised to give you the strength to meet any challenge. God has promised to lift you up and guide your steps if you let Him. God has promised that when you entrust your life to Him completely and without reservation, He will give you the courage to face any trial and the wisdom to live in His righteousness.

God's hand uplifts those who turn their hearts and prayers to Him. Will you count yourself among that number? Will you accept God's peace and wear God's armor against the temptations and distractions of our dangerous world? If you do, you can live courageously and optimistically, knowing that you have been forever touched by the loving, unfailing, uplifting hand of God.

Because He lives, I can face tomorrow; because He lives, all fear is gone; because I know He holds the future, and life is worth the living just because He lives.

Gloria Gaither and William J. Gaither

TODAY'S BIG IDEAS ABOUT GOLF AND LIFE

Each golfer ought to have a style which is the reflection of himself, his build, his mind, his age, and his previous habits.

Sir Walter Simpson

A divine strength is given to those who yield themselves to the Father and obey what He tells them to do.

Warren Wiersbe

When God is our strength, it is strength indeed; when our strength is our own, it is only weakness.

St. Augustine

A TIMELY TIP

Need strength? Slow down, get more rest, engage in sensible exercise, and turn your troubles over to God . . . but not necessarily in that order.

And He said to me, "My grace is sufficient for you, for My strength is made perfect in weakness."

2 Corinthians 12:9 NKJV

DAY 26

A BOOK UNLIKE
ANY OTHER

*For I am not ashamed of the gospel of Christ, for it is the
power of God to salvation for everyone who believes.*

The Bible can be a powerful tool for defeating stress. George Mueller observed, "The vigor of our spiritual lives will be in exact proportion to the place held by the Bible in our lives and in our thoughts." As Christians, we are called upon to study God's Holy Word and then apply it to our lives. When we do, we are blessed.

The Bible is a priceless gift, a tool for Christians to use as they share the Good News of their Savior, Christ Jesus. Too many Christians, however, keep their spiritual tool kits tightly closed and out of sight. Jonathan Edwards advised, "Be assiduous in reading the Holy Scriptures. This is the fountain whence all knowledge in divinity must be derived. Therefore let not this treasure lie by you neglected." God's Holy Word is, indeed, a priceless, one-of-a-kind treasure. Handle it with care, but, more importantly, handle it every day.

GREAT IDEAS FROM GOLFING GREATS

The facility for keeping oneself relaxed at all times adds a great deal to the pleasure of living.

Bobby Locke

The first step in building a solid, dependable attitude is to be realistic, not only about your inherent capabilities, but also about how well you are playing to those capabilities on any given day.

Byron Nelson

The mind messes up more shots than the body.

Tommy Bolt

A TIMELY TIP

God intends for you to use His Word as your guidebook for life . . . your intentions should be the same.

Every word of God is pure: he is a shield unto them that put their trust in him.

Proverbs 30:5 KJV

61

DAY 27

KEEP GROWING

Forsake foolishness and live, and go in the way of understanding.

Proverbs 9:6 NKJV

Complete spiritual maturity is never achieved in a day, or in a year, or even in a lifetime. The journey toward spiritual maturity is an ongoing process that continues, day by day, throughout every stage of life. Every stage of life has its opportunities and its challenges, and if we're wise, we continue to seek God's guidance as each new chapter of life unfolds.

From time to time, all of us encounter circumstances that test our faith. When we encounter life's inevitable tragedies, trials, uncertainties, and disappointments, we may be tempted to blame God or to rebel against Him. But the Bible reminds us that the trials of life should be viewed as opportunities for growth: "Consider it a great joy, my brothers, whenever you experience various trials, knowing that the testing of your faith produces endurance. But endurance must do its complete work, so that you may be mature and complete, lacking nothing" (James 1:2-4 HCSB)

Have you recently encountered one of life's inevitable tests? If so, remember that God still has lessons that He intends to teach you. So ask yourself this: what lesson is God trying to teach me today?

GREAT IDEAS FROM GOLFING GREATS

I try to put bad things that have happened to me out of my mind right away. Over as long a stretch as 54 or 72 holes of golf, similar misfortunes are sure to overtake virtually everyone else.

Nancy Lopez

It takes just as long to play your way out of a slump as it does to play your way into one.

Harvey Penick

No matter what happens, keep on hitting the ball.

Harry Vardon

✕ A TIMELY TIP ✕

When it comes to your faith, God doesn't intend for you to stand still. He wants you to keep moving and growing.

But grow in the grace and knowledge of our Lord and Savior Jesus Christ. To Him be the glory both now and to the day of eternity.

2 Peter 3:18 HCSB

CONSIDER
THE POSSIBILITIES

For nothing will be impossible with God.

Luke 1:37 HCSB

Are you afraid to ask God to do big things—or to make big changes—in your life? Is your faith threadbare and worn? If so, it's time to abandon your doubts and reclaim your faith in God's promises.

Ours is a God of infinite possibilities. But sometimes, because of limited faith and limited understanding, we wrongly assume that God cannot or will not intervene in the affairs of mankind. Such assumptions are simply wrong.

God's Holy Word makes it clear: absolutely nothing is impossible for the Lord. And since the Bible means what it says, you can be comforted in the knowledge that the Creator of the universe can do miraculous things in your own life and in the lives of your loved ones. Your challenge, as a believer, is to take God at His word, and to expect the miraculous.

God's faithfulness and grace make the impossible possible.

Sheila Walsh

TODAY'S BIG IDEAS ABOUT GOLF AND LIFE

To find a man's true character, play golf with him.

P. G. Wodehouse

Man's adversity is God's opportunity.

Matthew Henry

Jesus said to them, "I have shown you many great miracles from the Father."

John 10:32 NIV

TODAY'S SCORE CARD

Jot Down Your Thoughts About . . .
Your Biggest Dreams

_____

_____

_____

_____

_____

_____

_____

DAY 29

A LESSON ABOUT HARD WORK

Take a lesson from the ants, you lazybones. Learn from their ways and be wise! Even though they have no prince, governor, or ruler to make them work, they labor hard all summer, gathering food for the winter. But you, lazybones, how long will you sleep? When will you wake up?

Proverbs 6:6-9 NLT

Since the days of Adam and Eve, God has allowed His children to make choices for themselves, and so it is with you. You can either dig in and work hard, or you can retreat to the couch, click on the TV, and hope things get better on their own. Hard work is the best plan.

The Bible instructs us that we can learn an important lesson of a surprising source: ants. Ants are among nature's most industrious creatures. They do their work without supervision, rumination, or hesitation. We should do likewise. When times are tough, we must summon the courage and determination to work ourselves out of trouble.

God has created a world in which diligence is rewarded and sloth is not. So whatever you choose to do, do it with commitment, excitement, and vigor. God didn't create you for a life of mediocrity; He created you for far greater things. Reaching for greater things—and defeating tough times—usually requires work and lots of it, which is perfectly fine with God. After all, He knows that you're up to the task, and He still has big plans for you. Very big plans...

THE JOYS OF GOLF

Go out and have fun. Golf is a game for everyone, not just for the talented few.

Harvey Penick

Go play golf. Go to the golf course. Hit the ball. Find the ball. Repeat until the ball is in the hole. Have fun. The end.

Chuck Hogan

Golf courses are the answer to the world's problems. When I get out on that green carpet called a fairway and manage to poke the ball right down the middle, my surroundings look like a touch of heaven on earth.

Jimmy Demaret

TIME FOR RENEWAL

I will give you a new heart and put a new spirit within you.

Ezekiel 36:26 HCSB

Even the most inspired men and women can, from time to time, find themselves running on empty. The demands of daily life can drain us of our strength and rob us of the joy that is rightfully ours in Christ. When we find ourselves tired, discouraged, or worse, there is a source from which we can draw the power needed to recharge our spiritual batteries. That source is God.

God intends that His children lead joyous lives filled with abundance and peace. But sometimes, abundance and peace seem very far away. It is then that we must turn to God for renewal, and when we do, He will restore us.

Are you tired or troubled? Turn your heart toward God in prayer. Are you weak or worried? Take the time—or, more accurately, make the time—to read God's Word. When you do, you'll discover that the Creator of the universe stands always ready and always able to create a new sense of wonderment and joy in you.

He is the God of wholeness and restoration.

Stormie Omartian

THE JOYS OF GOLF

Take pleasure, not in the score, but in the game.

Bobby Jones

Relax. Enjoy the walk between shots. That's your chance to loosen up so your next shot is comfortable.

Julius Boros

I'm a golfaholic. And all the counseling in the world wouldn't help me.

Lee Trevino

✕ A TIMELY TIP ✕

God wants to give you peace, and He wants to renew your spirit. It's up to you to slow down and give Him a chance to do it.

The One who was sitting on the throne said, "Look! I am making everything new!" Then he said, "Write this, because these words are true and can be trusted."

Revelation 21:5 NCV

PESSIMISTS BEWARE

When doubts filled my mind, your comfort gave me renewed hope and cheer.

Psalm 94:19 NLT

Pessimists beware: The self-fulfilling prophecy lurks near every tee box, fairway and green. On the links, a negative attitude is the most dangerous hazard because it comes into play on every shot.

Perhaps no player, male or female, has ever enjoyed the self-assurance of Babe Didrikson Zaharias. She once addressed a crowd of reporters by saying, "Everybody come closer now. Today you're looking at the best." And Babe's words were not idle boasting; she backed them up on the golf course.

If your golfing psyche is in need of an attitude adjustment, the following quotations will help. As you learn to think positively about your game, you'll make the self-fulfilling prophecy your permanent playing partner. Together, the two of you will be a fabulous team.

We never get anywhere—nor do our conditions and circumstances change—when we look at the dark side of life.

Mrs. Charles E. Cowman

TODAY'S BIG IDEAS ABOUT GOLF AND LIFE

Maintaining composure on the golf course is worth at least three shots a round.

Billy Casper

God is still in the process of dispensing gifts, and He uses ordinary individuals like us to develop those gifts in other people.

Howard Hendricks

To lose heart is to lose everything.

John Eldredge

✕ A TIMELY TIP ✕

Pessimism and Christianity don't mix. If you genuinely believe that God is good and that His Son died for your sins, how can you be pessimistic about your future? The answer, of course, is that you can't!

———————————————

So encourage each other and give each other strength, just as you are doing now.

1 Thessalonians 5:11 NCV

THE STRUGGLE AGAINST WORLDLINESS

And do not be conformed to this world, but be transformed by the renewing of your mind, so that you may prove what the will of God is, that which is good and acceptable and perfect.

Romans 12:2 NASB

We live in the world, but we should not worship it—yet at every turn, or so it seems, we are tempted to do otherwise. As Warren Wiersbe correctly observed, "Because the world is deceptive, it is dangerous."

The 21st-century world we live in is a noisy, stress-filled, distracting place, a place that offers countless temptations and dangers. The world seems to cry, "Worship me with your time, your money, your energy, your thoughts, and your life!" But if we are wise, we won't fall prey to that temptation.

C. S. Lewis said, "Aim at heaven and you will get earth thrown in; aim at earth and you will get neither." That's good advice. You're likely to hit what you aim at, so aim high . . . aim at heaven.

GREAT IDEAS FROM GOLFING GREATS

Pop didn't just teach me golf. He taught me discipline.

Arnold Palmer

If you have discipline, you can relax and concentrate.

Sandra Haynie

The mental part of competitive golf is an overwhelmingly big part.

Nancy Lopez

✕ A TIMELY TIP ✕

Your world is full of distractions and temptations. Your challenge is to live in the world but not be of the world.

Pure and undefiled religion before our God and Father is this: to look after orphans and widows in their distress and to keep oneself unstained by the world.

James 1:27 HCSB

BEATING STRESS ONE DAY AT A TIME

This is the day the LORD has made; we will rejoice and be glad in it.

Psalm 118:24 NKJV

Just getting by in these turbulent times can be stressful, very stressful. You live in a world that is brimming with demands, distractions, and deadlines (not to mention temptations, timetables, requirements, and responsibilities). Whew! No wonder you may be stressed.

What can you do in response to the stressors of everyday life? A wonderful place to start is by turning things over to God.

Psalm 118:24 reminds us that this day, like every other, is a glorious gift from the Father. How will you use that gift? Will you celebrate it and use it for His purposes? If so, you'll discover that when you turn things over to Him—when you allow God to rule over every corner of your life—He will calm your fears and guide your steps.

So today, make sure that you focus on God and upon His will for your life. Then, ask for His help. And remember: No challenge is too great for Him. Not even yours.

GREAT IDEAS FROM GOLFING GREATS

What other people may find in poetry or art museums, I find in the flight of a good drive.

Arnold Palmer

I expect to play golf until I am 90—even longer if anybody figures out a way to swing a club from a rocking chair.

Babe Didrikson Zaharias

You're never too old to play golf. If you can walk, you can play.

Louise Suggs

✕ A TIMELY TIP ✕

If you're energy is low or your nerves are frazzled, perhaps you need to slow down and have a heart-to-heart talk with God. And while you're at it, remember that God is bigger than your problems . . . much bigger.

Cast your burden on the Lord, and He shall sustain you; He shall never permit the righteous to be moved.

Psalm 55:22 NKJV

THE MORNING WATCH

Every morning he wakes me. He teaches me to listen like a student. The Lord God helps me learn...

Isaiah 50:4-5 NCV

Each new day is a gift from God, and if you are wise, you will spend a few quiet moments each morning thanking the Giver. When you do, you'll discover that time spent with God can lift your spirits and relieve your stress.

Warren Wiersbe writes, "Surrender your mind to the Lord at the beginning of each day." And that's sound advice. When you begin each day with your head bowed and your heart lifted, you are reminded of God's love, His protection, and His commandments. Then, you can align your priorities for the coming day with the teachings and commandments that God has placed upon your heart.

So, if you've acquired the unfortunate habit of trying to "squeeze" God into the corners of your life, it's time to reshuffle the items on your to-do list by placing God first. And if you haven't already done so, form the habit of spending quality time with your Father in heaven. He deserves it . . . and so do you.

GREAT IDEAS FROM GOLFING GREATS

Dare to play your own game.

Annika Sorenstam

More matches are lost through carelessness at the beginning than any other cause.

Harry Vardon

The best advice I can give any golfer about playing fairway shots is: Don't be greedy.

Gary Player

TODAY'S SCORE CARD

Jot Down Your Thoughts About . . .
Reasons to Be Thankful

THE RIGHT PRIORITIES

We can't afford to waste a minute, must not squander these precious daylight hours in frivolity and indulgence, in sleeping around and dissipation, in bickering and grabbing everything in sight. Get out of bed and get dressed! Don't loiter and linger, waiting until the very last minute. Dress yourselves in Christ, and be up and about!

Romans 13:13-14 MSG

Have you fervently asked God to help prioritize your life? Have you asked Him for guidance and for the courage to do the things that you know need to be done? If so, then you're continually inviting your Creator to reveal Himself in a variety of ways. As a follower of Christ, you must do no less.

When you make God's priorities your priorities, you will receive God's abundance and His peace. When you make God a full partner in every aspect of your life, He will lead you along the proper path: His path. When you allow God to reign over your heart, He will honor you with spiritual blessings that are simply too numerous to count. So, as you plan for the day ahead, make God's will your ultimate priority. When you do, every other priority will have a tendency to fall neatly into place.

TODAY'S BIG IDEAS ABOUT GOLF AND LIFE

Golf may not teach character, but it reveals it.

Thomas Boswell

Blessed are those who know what on earth they are here on earth to do and set themselves about the business of doing it.

Max Lucado

The thing you should want most is God's kingdom and doing what God wants. Then all these other things you need will be given to you.

Matthew 6:33 NCV

TODAY'S SCORE CARD

Jot Down Your Thoughts About . . .
Your Most Important Priorities

_____

_____

_____

_____

_____

_____

CONTROLLING YOUR EMOTIONS

Don't turn your back on wisdom, for she will protect you. Love her, and she will guard you.

Proverbs 4:6 NLT

Who is in charge of your emotions? Is it you, or have you formed the unfortunate habit of letting other people—or stressful situations—determine the quality of your thoughts and the direction of your day? If you're wise—and if you'd like to build a better life for yourself and your loved ones—you'll learn to control your emotions before your emotions control you.

Human emotions are highly variable, decidedly unpredictable, and often unreliable. Our emotions are like the weather, only far more fickle. So we must learn to live by faith, not by the ups and downs of our own emotional roller coasters.

Sometime during this day, you will probably be gripped by a strong negative feeling. Distrust it. Reign it in. Test it. And turn it over to God. Your emotions will inevitably change; God will not. So trust Him completely as you watch those negative feelings slowly evaporate into thin air—which, of course, they will.

PERFECTING YOUR PUTTING

The best putters are the breezy and optimistic people. Poor putters, by contrast, seem to be cranky and cantankerous characters.

Tony Lema

Practice three- and four-footers twice as much as you practice long putts.

Billy Casper

You can tell a good putt by the noise it makes.

Bobby Locke

✕ A TIMELY TIP ✕

Remember: Your life shouldn't be ruled by your emotions—your life should be ruled by God. So if you think you've lost control over your emotions, don't make big decisions, don't strike out against anybody, and don't speak out in anger. Count to ten (or more) and take "time out" from your situation until you calm down.

Peace I leave with you; My peace I give to you; not as the world gives do I give to you. Do not let your heart be troubled, nor let it be fearful.

John 14:27 NASB

81

THE POWER OF PERSEVERANCE

For a righteous man may fall seven times and rise again.

Proverbs 24:16 NKJV

The game of golf teaches us that perseverance is eventually rewarded, both on the course and off. The next time you find your determination tested to the limit, remember that God is as near as your next breath, and remember that He offers strength and comfort to His children. He is your shield and your strength; He is your protector and your deliverer. Call upon Him in your hour of need and then be comforted. Whatever your challenge, whatever your trouble, God can help you persevere.

Perhaps you are in a hurry for God to help you resolve your difficulties. Perhaps you're anxious to earn the victories that you feel you've already earned from life. Perhaps you're drumming your fingers, impatiently waiting for God to act. If so, be forewarned: God operates on His own timetable, not yours. Sometimes, God may answer your prayers with silence, and when He does, you must patiently persevere. In times of trouble, you must remain steadfast and trust in the merciful goodness of your Heavenly Father. Whatever your problem, He can handle it. Your job is to keep persevering until He does.

TODAY'S BIG IDEAS ABOUT GOLF AND LIFE

You tend to get impatient with less-than-perfect shots, but you have to remember that less-than-perfect shots win Opens.

Curtis Strange

Stand still and refuse to retreat. Look at it as God looks at it and draw upon his power to hold up under the blast.

Charles Swindoll

Just remember, every flower that ever bloomed had to go through a whole lot of dirt to get there!

Barbara Johnson

✕ A TIMELY TIP ✕

If you want to be a champion, you can't give up at the first sign of trouble. So if at first you don't succeed, keep trying until you do.

Patient endurance is what you need now, so you will continue to do God's will. Then you will receive all that he has promised.

Hebrews 10:36 NLT

83

GETTING ENOUGH REST?

Come to me, all you who are weary and burdened, and I will give you rest. Take my yoke upon you and learn from me, for I am gentle and humble in heart, and you will find rest for your souls. For my yoke is easy and my burden is light.

Matthew 11:28-30 NIV

Physical exhaustion is God's way of telling us to slow down. God expects us to work hard, of course, but He also intends for us to rest. When we fail to take the rest that we need, we do a disservice to ourselves and to our families.

We live in a world that tempts us to stay up late—very late. But too much late-night TV, combined with too little sleep, is a prescription for exhaustion.

Each of us bears a personal responsibility for the general state of our own physical health. Certainly, various aspects of health are beyond our control: illness sometimes strikes even the healthiest men and women. But for most of us, physical health is a choice: it is the result of hundreds of small decisions that we make every day of our lives. If we make decisions that promote good health, our bodies respond. But if we fall into bad habits and undisciplined lifestyles, we suffer tragic consequences.

Are your physical or spiritual batteries running low? Is your energy on the wane? Are your emotions frayed? If so, it's time to turn your thoughts and your prayers to God's Son. And when you're finished, it's probably time to turn off the lights and go to bed!

THE JOYS OF GOLF

There is nothing like stepping onto a golf course on a clear fresh morning.

Kathy Whitworth

Try to find something joyful about each round of golf.

Patty Sheehan

TODAY'S SCORE CARD

Jot Down Your Thoughts About . . .
The Amount of Sleep That's Right for You

SAYING YES TO GOD

Cast your burden upon the Lord and He will sustain you: He will never allow the righteous to be shaken.

Psalm 55:22 NASB

Your decision to seek a deeper relationship with God will not remove all problems from your life; to the contrary, it will bring about a series of personal crises as you constantly seek to say "yes" to God although the world encourages you to do otherwise. You live in a world that seeks to snare your attention and lead you away from God. Each time you are tempted to distance yourself from the Creator, you will face a spiritual crisis. A few of these crises may be monumental in scope, but most will be the small, everyday decisions of life. In fact, life here on earth can be seen as one test after another—and with each crisis comes yet another opportunity to grow closer to God . . . or to distance yourself from His plan for your life.

Today, you will face many opportunities to say "yes" to your Creator—and you will also encounter many opportunities to say "no" to Him. Your answers will determine the quality of your day and the direction of your life, so answer carefully . . . very carefully.

GREAT IDEAS FROM GOLFING GREATS

After you've grooved your swing, you still have to master the tactics of getting around the course. A good swing is small satisfaction if you can't break 100.

Sam Snead

In every case, there is a risk-reward factor. The course forces you to evaluate each shot in terms of nerve and skill. The more decisive your shot selection and thought process, the greater your chances of mastering the course.

Robert Trent Jones, Jr.

Play your own game. You can't be something you're not.

David Duval

✕ A TIMELY TIP ✕

If you're facing a crisis, don't face it alone. Enlist God's help. And then, when you've finished praying about your problem, don't be afraid to seek help from family, from friends, or from your pastor.

If anyone would come after me, he must deny himself and take up his cross and follow me.

Mark 8:34 NIV

EMBRACING YOUR FUTURE

*Don't brashly announce what you're going to do tomorrow;
you don't know the first thing about tomorrow.*

Proverbs 27:1 MSG

Sometimes the future seems bright, and sometimes it does not. Yet even when we cannot see the possibilities of tomorrow, God can. Our challenge is to trust ourselves to do the best work we can, and then to trust God to do the rest.

When we trust God, we should trust Him without reservation. We should steel ourselves against the inevitable disappointments of the day, secure in the knowledge that our Heavenly Father has a plan for the future that is brighter than we can imagine.

Are you willing to look to the future with trust and confidence? Hopefully so, because the future should not to be feared, it should be embraced. And it most certainly should be embraced by you.

Hoping for a good future without investing in today is like a farmer waiting for a crop without ever planting any seed.

John Maxwell

GREAT IDEAS FROM GOLFING GREATS

Every hole is a little tournament of its own.

Tom Watson

Don't just play your way around the course. Think your way around the course.

Sam Snead

Every golfer scores better when he learns his capabilities.

Tommy Armour

✕ A TIMELY TIP ✕

Your future depends, to a very great extent, upon you. So keep learning and keep growing personally, intellectually, emotionally, and spiritually.

For I know the thoughts that I think toward you, says the Lord, thoughts of peace and not of evil, to give you a future and a hope. Then you will call upon Me and go and pray to Me, and I will listen to you.

Jeremiah 29:11-12 NKJV

89

OUT OF BALANCE?

Grow a wise heart—you'll do yourself a favor; keep a clear head—you'll find a good life.

Proverbs 19:8 MSG

Life is a delicate balancing act, a tightrope walk with over-commitment on one side and under-commitment on the other. And it's up to each of us to walk carefully on that rope, not falling prey to pride (which causes us to attempt too much) or to fear (which causes us to attempt too little).

God's Word promises us the possibility of abundance (John 10:10). And we are far more likely to experience that abundance when we lead balanced lives.

Are you doing too much—or too little? If so, it's time to have a little chat with God. And if you listen carefully to His instructions, you will strive to achieve a more balanced life, a life that's right for you and your loved ones. When you do, everybody wins.

We are all created differently. We share a common need to balance the different parts of our lives.

Dr. Walt Larimore

PERFECTING YOUR PUTTING

All good putters have balance.

Arnold Palmer

All good putters hit the ball solidly.

Cary Middlecoff

Consistent skill around the greens is the biggest asset a golfer can have.

Gay Brewer

✕ A TIMELY TIP ✕

Life is a balancing act. To improve your balance, consult your heavenly Father many times each day.

Come to Me, all you who labor and are heavy laden, and I will give you rest. Take My yoke upon you and learn from Me, for I am gentle and lowly in heart, and you will find rest for your souls. For My yoke is easy and My burden is light.

Matthew 11:28-30 NKJV

CONCENTRATION IS ESSENTIAL

Keep your eyes focused on what is right, and look straight ahead to what is good.

Proverbs 4:25 NCV

You've heard the golf cliché on countless occasions: "Keep your head down." Since the better part of golf is played between the ears, it's no accident that the game's most popular adage concerns the human head. All golfers, from time to time, fall prey to the powerful temptation to look up before the swing is completed. The results are predictable: Curiosity kills the cat, or, in this case, the birdie.

In golf, as in life, concentration is rewarded at every turn. When we attend to the job at hand, the game seems to flow. But as distractions increase, so do bogeys.

If you're looking for a surefire way to lower your handicap, learn the fine art of concentration. If you keep your head down during the swing, you can probably hold your head high after the swing is over.

It is important to set goals because if you do not have a plan, a goal, a direction, a purpose, and a focus, you are not going to accomplish anything for the glory of God.

Bill Bright

PERFECTING YOUR PUTTING

Being free of doubt is just as necessary on a short putt as any other shot.

Harvey Penick

Concentrate on the things you need to do to make a putt, not on the consequences if you miss.

Kathy Whitworth

Don't be a negative putter.

Billy Casper

TODAY'S SCORE CARD

Jot Down Your Thoughts About . . .
The Importance of Concentration

SWING EASY,
HIT HARD

Depend on the Lord and his strength; always go to him for help. Remember the miracles he has done; remember his wonders and his decisions.

Psalm 105:4-5 NCV

In golf, power is paradoxical. Overswinging destroys both balance and tempo, resulting in decreased accuracy and distance. In the tee box, the law of unintended consequences is alive and well: When we swing too hard, our shots fall short.

Recalling his days on the tour, Byron Nelson noted, "We thought that strength denied touch and that you could not consistently hit the ball long and straight. It's been proved that you can."

The purpose of a golf swing is to develop clubhead speed through the point of impact. This goal is best achieved through smooth acceleration, not quick bursts of energy.

The same principles that provide power on the golf course also make us more effective in other areas of our lives. Life, like that little dimpled golf ball, can't be overpowered. So the best course of action, no matter where we find ourselves, is to swing easy and hit hard.

IMPROVING YOUR SWING

Golf is a game based not only on an intellectual understanding but also on sensitivity for the instrument. You can't bully your way to a good golf swing.

Jim Flick

Overswinging does not produce power.

Judy Rankin

If you want to hit it farther, hit it better.

Jack Nicklaus

✕ A TIMELY TIP ✕

Need strength? Slow down, get more rest, engage in sensible exercise, and—most importantly—turn your troubles over to God.

No rotten talk should come from your mouth, but only what is good for the building up of someone in need, in order to give grace to those who hear.

Ephesians 4:29 HCSB

95

A DOSE OF LAUGHTER

A happy heart is like good medicine.

Proverbs 17:22 NCV

Laughter is medicine for the soul (not to mention a fabulous stress-reducer), but sometimes, amid the challenges of the day, we forget to take our medicine. Instead of viewing our world with a mixture of optimism and humor, we allow worries and distractions to rob us of the joy that God intends for our lives.

So the next time you find yourself dwelling upon the negatives of life, refocus your attention to things positive. If you find yourself thinking pessimistically about a shot gone bad or missing a putt, stop yourself and turn your thoughts around. And, if you see your glass as "half empty," rest assured that your spiritual vision is impaired. With God, your glass is never half empty. With God as your protector and Christ as your Savior, your glass is filled to the brim and overflowing . . . forever.

Today, as you go about your daily activities, approach the game of life with a smile. After all, God created laughter for a reason . . . and Father indeed knows best. So laugh!

TODAY'S BIG IDEAS ABOUT GOLF AND LIFE

If you want people to feel comfortable around you, to enjoy being with you, then learn to laugh at yourself and find humor in life's little mishaps.

Dennis Swanberg

In our tense, uptight society where folks are rushing to make appointments they have already missed, a good laugh can be as refreshing as a cup of cold water in the desert.

Barbara Johnson

I know I am getting better at golf because I am hitting fewer spectators.

Gerald Ford

✕ A TIMELY TIP ✕

Life has a lighter side—look for it, especially when times are tough.

There is a time for everything, and a season for every activity under heaven . . . a time to weep and a time to laugh, a time to mourn and a time to dance . . . .

Ecclesiastes 3:1,4 NIV

97

DAY 45

GOD KEEPS
HIS PROMISES

Cast your burden upon the Lord and He will sustain you: He will never allow the righteous to be shaken.

Psalm 55:22 NASB

On the golf course, or away from it, all of us face adversity, discouragement, and occasional disappointments. When we are troubled, we can call upon God, and, in His own time and according to His own plan, He will heal us.

Times of adversity can also be times of intense personal and spiritual growth. In difficult times, we learn lessons that we could have learned in no other way: We learn about life, we learn about ourselves, and we learn about God's ability to renew our spirits and restore our strength.

Are you anxious? Take those anxieties to God. Are you troubled? Take your troubles to Him. Does your world seem to be trembling beneath your feet? Seek protection from the One who cannot be moved. The same God who created the universe will protect you if you ask Him . . . so ask Him.

PERFECTING YOUR PUTTING

The real road to improvement lies in gaining a working knowledge of the correct swing in general, and yours in particular.

Bobby Jones

Your putter is the most important club in your bag.

Harvey Penick

Attitude is more important on the greens than anywhere else on the golf course.

Gay Brewer

✕ A TIMELY TIP ✕

Change is inevitable; growth is not. God will come to your doorstep on countless occasions with opportunities to learn and to grow. And He will knock. Your challenge, of course, is to open the door.

Therefore do not worry about tomorrow, for tomorrow will worry about itself. Each day has enough trouble of its own.

Matthew 6:34 NIV

THE POWER OF POSITIVE GOLF

My cup runs over. Surely goodness and mercy shall follow me all the days of my life; and I will dwell in the house of the Lord Forever.

Psalm 23:5-6 NKJV

Are you an optimistic golfer and an enthusiastic Christian? You should be. After all, you have every reason to be optimistic about life here on earth and life eternal.

As C. H. Spurgeon observed, "Our hope in Christ for the future is the mainstream of our joy." But sometimes, you may find yourself pulled down by the inevitable demands and worries of life here on earth. If you find yourself discouraged, stressed, or both, then it's time to take your concerns to God. When you do, He will lift your spirits and renew your strength.

Today think optimistically about your life, your profession, your family, your future, and your golf game. Trust your hopes, not your fears. Take time to celebrate God's glorious creation. And then, when you've filled your heart with hope and gladness, share your optimism with others. They'll be better for it, and so will you.

TODAY'S BIG IDEAS ABOUT GOLF AND LIFE

In choosing a partner, always pick the optimist.

Tony Lema

Go forward confidently, energetically attacking problems, expecting favorable outcomes.

Norman Vincent Peale

Make the least of all that goes and the most of all that comes. Don't regret what is past. Cherish what you have. Look forward to all that is to come. And most important of all, rely moment by moment on Jesus Christ.

Gigi Graham Tchividjian

✕ A TIMELY TIP ✕

Optimism pays. Pessimism does not. Guard your thoughts and plan your shots accordingly.

The Lord is my light and my salvation; whom shall I fear? The Lord is the strength of my life; of whom shall I be afraid?

Psalm 27:1 KJV

WORRIED?

Give your worries to the Lord, and he will take care of you.
He will never let good people down.

Psalm 55:22 NCV

The best golfers find ways to concentrate more and worry less. But sometimes, it's hard not to worry. At times, we may find ourselves fretting over the countless details of everyday life. We may worry about our relationships, our finances, our health, or any number of potential problems, some large and some small.

If you're a "worrier" by nature, it's probably time to rethink the way that you think. Perhaps you've formed the unfortunate habit of focusing too intently on negative aspects of life while spending too little time counting your blessings. If so, take your worries to God . . . and leave them there. When you do, you'll learn to worry a little less and to trust God a little more—and that's as it should be because God is trustworthy, you are protected, and your future can be intensely bright.

Things can be very difficult for us, but nothing is too hard for Him.

Charles Stanley

GREAT IDEAS FROM GOLFING GREATS

Being in control on a golf course means making intelligent decisions—knowing when to be aggressive and when to be cautious.

Curtis Strange

The guys who do well are the ones with the strongest mental outlook.

Justin Leonard

It is not mere technical skill that makes a man a golfer, it is the golfing soul.

P. G. Wodehouse

TODAY'S SCORE CARD

Jot Down Your Thoughts About . . .
The Futility of Worry

CONFIDENCE RESTORED

I've told you all this so that trusting me, you will be unshakable and assured, deeply at peace. In this godless world you will continue to experience difficulties. But take heart! I've conquered the world.

John 16:33 MSG

Are you a confident, fully engaged player in the game of life, or do you live under a cloud of uncertainty and doubt? As a Christian, you have many reasons to be confident. After all, God is in His heaven; Christ has risen; and you are the recipient of God's grace. Despite these blessings, you may, from time to time, find yourself being tormented by stressful, destructive emotions—and you are certainly not alone.

During turbulent times like these, even the most faithful Christians are overcome by occasional bouts of fear and doubt. And you are no different. But even when you feel very distant from God, remember that God is never distant from you. When you sincerely seek His presence, He will touch your heart, calm your fears, and restore your confidence.

PERFECTING YOUR PUTTING

If you contact the sweet spot every time, you'll be on the way to solid putting.

Lee Trevino

Practice the really important putts: the five and six-footers.

Nancy Lopez

Imagine there's a second ball placed two inches (toward the target) in front of the real one. Now, accelerate the putterhead smoothly through the imaginary ball, sending it straight into the hole.

Fred Couples

✕ A TIMELY TIP ✕

If you want to be a winner, you must train yourself to think like one. You need confidence in yourself, your abilities, your future, and your Creator.

Be strong and courageous, and do the work. Don't be afraid or discouraged by the size of the task, for the LORD God, my God, is with you. He will not fail you or forsake you.

1 Chronicles 28:20 NLT

STAYING IN CONTROL

So prepare your minds for service and have self-control. All your hope should be for the gift of grace that will be yours when Jesus Christ is shown to you.

1 Peter 1:13 NCV

On the golf course, self-control is essential. And, self-control pays big dividends in life, too. God's Word is clear: we are called to lead lives of discipline, diligence, moderation, and maturity. But the world often tempts us to do otherwise. Everywhere we turn, or so it seems, we are faced with powerful temptations to behave in undisciplined ways—but God has far better plans for our days and for our lives.

God's Word instructs us to be disciplined in our thoughts and our actions; God's Word warns us against the dangers of impulsive behavior.

Do you seek to reap the rewards that God offers those who lead disciplined lives? If so, then you must learn to discipline yourself . . . before God does.

Man's great danger is the combination of his increased control over the elements and his lack of control over himself.

Albert Schweitzer

TODAY'S BIG IDEAS ABOUT GOLF AND LIFE

In golf, loss of self-control is reflected in poor decision-making.

Curtis Strange

The alternative to discipline is disaster.

Vance Havner

Your thoughts are the determining factor as to whose mold you are conformed to. Control your thoughts and you control the direction of your life.

Charles Stanley

✕ A TIMELY TIP ✕

To be successful in the game of life (or, for that matter, in the game of golf), you must learn the importance of self-discipline and self-control. The sooner you learn how to control yourself, the sooner you'll start winning.

Do you not know that those who run in a race all run, but only one receives the prize? Run in such a way that you may win. Everyone who competes in the games exercises self-control in all things.

1 Corinthians 9:24-25 NASB

HE OVERCOMES

These things I have spoken to you, that in Me you may have peace. In the world you will have tribulation; but be of good cheer, I have overcome the world.

John 16:33 NKJV

The hope that the world offers is fleeting and imperfect. The hope that God offers is unchanging, unshakable, and unending. It is no wonder, then, that when we seek security from worldly sources, our hopes are often dashed and our stresses are often increased. Thankfully, God has no such record of failure.

Where will you place your hopes today? Will you entrust your future to man or to God? Will you seek solace exclusively from fallible human beings, or will you place your hopes, first and foremost, in the trusting hands of your Creator? The decision is yours, and you must live with the results of the choice you make.

For thoughtful believers, hope begins with God. Period. So today, as you embark upon the next stage of your life's journey, consider the words of the Psalmist: "You are my hope; O Lord GOD, You are my confidence" (71:5 NASB). Then, place your trust in the One who cannot be shaken.

TODAY'S BIG IDEAS ABOUT GOLF AND LIFE

The philosophy of "think positive" is essential for winning golf.

Nancy Lopez

We create success or failure on the course primarily through our thoughts.

Gary Player

Don't worry. Just leave everything in the hands of God.

Babe Didrikson Zaharias

✕ A TIMELY TIP ✕

If you're experiencing hard times, you'll be wise to start spending more time with God. And if you do your part, God will do His part. So never be afraid to hope—or to ask—for a miracle.

Be of good courage, and he shall strengthen your heart, all ye that hope in the LORD.

Psalm 31:24 KJV

NEIGHBORS IN NEED

Each one of us needs to look after the good of the people around us, asking ourselves, "How can I help?" That's exactly what Jesus did.

Romans 15:2-3 MSG

We know that we're instructed to love our neighbors, and yet there's so little time . . . and we're so busy. No matter. As Christians, we are commanded by our Lord and Savior Jesus Christ to love our neighbors just as we love ourselves. Period.

This very day, you will encounter someone who needs a word of encouragement, or a pat on the back, or a helping hand, or a heartfelt prayer. And, if you don't reach out to your friend, who will? If you don't take the time to understand the needs of your neighbors, who will? If you don't love your brothers and sisters, who will? So, today, look for a neighbor in need . . . and then do something to help. Father's orders.

That's a good part of the good old days—to be genuinely interested in your neighbor, and if you hear a distress signal, go see about him and his problem.

Jerry Clower

TODAY'S BIG IDEAS ABOUT GOLF AND LIFE

A couple of hours of practice is worth ten sloppy rounds.

Babe Didrikson Zaharias

Make it a rule, and pray to God to help you to keep it, never, if possible, to lie down at night without being able to say: "I have made one human being at least a little wiser, or a little happier, or at least a little better this day."

Charles Kingsley

When we have the opportunity to help anyone, we should do it. But we should give special attention to those who are in the family of believers.

Galatians 6:10 NCV

TODAY'S SCORE CARD

Jot Down Your Thoughts About . . .
People Who Need Your Help Today

BEYOND ENVY

Therefore, laying aside all malice, all deceit, hypocrisy, envy, and all evil speaking, as newborn babes, desire the pure milk of the word, that you may grow thereby.

1 Peter 2:1-2 NKJV

Because we are frail, imperfect human beings, we are sometimes envious of others. But God's Word warns us that envy is self-destructive. Thus, we must guard ourselves against the natural tendency to feel resentment and jealousy when other people experience good fortune, on the links, or off.

As Christians, we have absolutely no reason to be envious of any people on earth. After all, we are already recipients of the greatest gift in all creation: God's grace. We have been promised the gift of eternal life through God's only begotten Son, and we must count that gift as our most precious possession.

So here's a simple suggestion that is guaranteed to bring you happiness: fill your heart with God's love, God's promises, and God's Son . . . and when you do so, leave no room for envy, hatred, bitterness, or regret.

How can you possess the miseries of envy when you possess in Christ the best of all portions?

C. H. Spurgeon

PERFECTING YOUR PUTTING

Putting is like wisdom—partly a natural gift and partly the accumulation of experience.

Arnold Palmer

Putting is mental. You must put the fear of failure out of your mind.

Harvey Penick

Putting is more than half the game.

Arnold Palmer

 **A TIMELY TIP**

Feelings of envy rob you of happiness and peace. So, don't rob yourself.

A tranquil heart is life to the body, but jealousy is rottenness to the bones.

Proverbs 14:30 HCSB

INFINITE POSSIBILITIES

Is anything too hard for the LORD?

Genesis 18:14 KJV

Are you afraid to ask God to do big things in your life? If so, it's time to abandon your doubts and reclaim your faith in God's promises.

Ours is a God of infinite possibilities. But sometimes, because of limited faith and limited understanding, we wrongly assume that God cannot or will not intervene in the affairs of mankind. Such assumptions are simply wrong.

God's Holy Word makes it clear: absolutely nothing is impossible for the Lord. And since the Bible means what it says, you can be comforted in the knowledge that the Creator of the universe can do miraculous things in your own life and in the lives of your loved ones. Your challenge, as a believer, is to take God at His word, and to expect the miraculous.

God is the silent partner in all great enterprises.

Abraham Lincoln

GREAT IDEAS FROM GOLFING GREATS

Great players concentrate on cause rather than result.

Cary Middlecoff

Imagine what you want to do, not what you don't want to do.

Sandra Haynie

Most golfers prepare for disaster. A good golfer prepares for success.

Bob Toski

✕ A TIMELY TIP ✕

Focus on possibilities. Of course you will encounter hazards from time to time, but, don't invest large quantities of your life focusing on past misfortunes. In the game of life, regret is a losing strategy.

Ah, Lord God! Behold, You have made the heavens and the earth by Your great power and outstretched arm. There is nothing too hard for You.

Jeremiah 32:17 NKJV

115

CONTAGIOUS FAITH

Whatever you do, work at it with all your heart, as working for the Lord, not for men.

Colossians 3:23 NIV

The stronger your faith, the better you can rise above the inevitable stresses of turbulent times. And the more enthused you are about your faith, the better you can share it.

Are you genuinely excited about your faith? And do you make your enthusiasm known to those around you? Or are you a "silent ambassador" for Christ? God's preference is clear: He intends that you stand before others and proclaim your faith.

Genuine, heartfelt Christianity is contagious. If you enjoy a life-altering relationship with God, that relationship will have an impact on others—perhaps a profound impact.

Does Christ reign over your life? Then share your testimony and your excitement. The world needs both.

Your enthusiasm will be infectious, stimulating, and attractive to others. They will love you for it. They will go for you and with you.

Norman Vincent Peale

PERFECTING YOUR PUTTING

The golfer who tries to hole all his putts is usually the one with the most three-putts.

Sam Snead

The things that hurt my putting the most when it was bad—and it was very bad at times—was thinking too much.

Bobby Jones

If you concentrate on making the putt, you'll find it hard to figure out ways to miss it.

Gay Brewer

✕ A TIMELY TIP ✕

If you're hesitant to talk about your faith, remember this: the greatest gift you can give a friend is the willingness to share your own personal testimony.

Never be lacking in zeal, but keep your spiritual fervor, serving the Lord.

Romans 12:11 NIV

FINDING REAL FULLFILLMENT

For You, O God, have tested us; You have refined us as silver is refined . . . we went through fire and through water; but You brought us out to rich fulfillment.

Psalm 66:10–12 NKJV

Everywhere we turn, or so it seems, the world promises fulfillment, contentment, and happiness. But the contentment that the world offers is fleeting and incomplete. Thankfully, the fulfillment that God offers is all encompassing and everlasting.

Sometimes, amid the inevitable hustle and bustle of life-here-on-earth, we can forfeit—albeit temporarily—the joy of Christ as we wrestle with the challenges of daily living. Yet God's Word is clear: fulfillment through Christ is available to all who seek it and claim it. Count yourself among that number. Seek first a personal, transforming relationship with Jesus, and then claim the joy, the fulfillment, and the spiritual abundance that the Shepherd offers His sheep.

We are never more fulfilled than when our longing for God is met by His presence in our lives.

Billy Graham

GREAT IDEAS FROM GOLFING GREATS

Accept your disappointments and triumphs equally.

Harvey Penick

A bogey can be like a wake-up call. It can snap you back mentally.

Peter Jacobsen

You can talk strategy all you want, but what really matters is resiliency.

Hale Irwin

✕ A TIMELY TIP ✕

Want to increase your sense of fulfillment? Then strive to find God's path for your life . . . and follow it.

May Your faithful love comfort me, as You promised Your servant.

Psalm 119:76 HCSB

CHRIST'S ABUNDANCE

I have come that they may have life, and that they may have it more abundantly.

John 10:10 NKJV

The familiar words of John 10:10 convey this promise: Jesus came to this earth so that you might have a life of abundance. Thankfully for Christians, our Savior's abundance is both spiritual and eternal; it never falters—even if we do—and it never dies. We need only to open our hearts to Him, and His grace becomes ours.

The spiritual abundance that Jesus promises is, indeed, available to you. Do you sincerely seek the riches that our Savior offers to those who give themselves to Him? Then follow Him completely and obey Him without reservation. Follow Him today, tomorrow, and every day that you live. When you do, you will receive the love and the abundance that He has promised.

Seek first the personal transformation that is available through a genuine relationship with Christ, and then claim the joy, the peace, and the spiritual abundance that the Shepherd offers His sheep.

Jesus wants Life for us, Life with a capital L.

John Eldredge

IMPROVING YOUR SWING

Correct one fault at a time. Concentrate on the one fault you want to overcome.

Sam Snead

I don't swing hard. I hit hard.

Julius Boros

A simple tip to improve timing is this: Pause briefly at the top of the backswing.

Tommy Armour

TODAY'S SCORE CARD

Jot Down Your Thoughts About . . .
What Abundance Really Means

GOD GUIDES US THROUGH TURBULENT TIMES

The steps of the Godly are directed by God. He delights in every detail of their lives.

Psalm 37:22 NLT

The Bible promises that God will guide you if you let Him. Your job, of course, is to let Him. But sometimes, you will be tempted to do otherwise. Sometimes, you'll be tempted to go along with the crowd; other times, you'll be tempted to do things your way, not God's way. When you feel those temptations, resist them.

What will you allow to guide you through the coming day: your own desires (or, for that matter, the desires of your friends)? Or will you allow God to lead the way? The answer should be obvious. You should let God be your guide. When you entrust your life to Him completely and without reservation, God will give you the strength to meet any challenge, the courage to face any trial, and the wisdom to live in His righteousness. So trust Him today and seek His guidance. When you do, your next step will be the right one.

GREAT IDEAS FROM GOLFING GREATS

Once a time is past, it's past. I have to look to the future. I have to see what skills I have now. I can't look backwards, because that man doesn't exist anymore.

Jack Nicklaus

To play competitive golf you must be determined, yet resigned.

Thomas Boswell

We must all play the ball as we find it.

Bobby Jones

✕ A TIMELY TIP ✕

Golf has rules and so does God. When you obey God's rules, you win; when you ignore God's rules, you lose. It's as simple as that.

_____

The true children of God are those who let God's Spirit lead them.

Romans 8:14 NCV

KEEPING UP WITH THE JONESES?

Wherever your treasure is, there your heart and thoughts will also be.

Luke 12:34 NLT

As a member-in-good-standing in this highly competitive, 21st-century world, you know that the demands and expectations of everyday living can seem burdensome, even overwhelming at times. Keeping up with the Joneses can become a full-time job if you let it. A better strategy, of course, is to stop trying to please the neighbors and to concentrate, instead, upon pleasing God.

Perhaps you have set your goals high; if so, congratulations! You're willing to dream big dreams, and that's a very good thing. But as you consider your life's purpose, don't allow your quest for excellence to interfere with the spiritual journey that God has planned for you.

As a believer, your instructions are clear: you must strive to please God. How do you please Him? By accepting His Son and obeying His commandments. All other concerns—including, but not limited to, keeping up with the Joneses—are of little or no importance.

GREAT IDEAS FROM GOLFING GREATS

You might as well praise a man for not robbing a bank as to praise him for playing by the rules.

Bobby Jones

What difference does it make to you what someone else becomes, or says, or does? You do not need to answer for others, only for yourself.

Thomas à Kempis

Do not be misled: "Bad company corrupts good character."

1 Corinthians 15:33 NIV

TODAY'S SCORE CARD

Jot Down Your Thoughts About . . .
The Dangers of Too Much Peer Pressure

_____

_____

_____

_____

_____

_____

DAY 59

A WORTHY DISCIPLE

He has showed you, O man, what is good. And what does the LORD require of you? To act justly and to love mercy and to walk humbly with your God.

Micah 6:8 NIV

When Jesus addressed His disciples, He warned that each one must, "take up his cross and follow me." The disciples must have known exactly what the Master meant. In Jesus' day, prisoners were forced to carry their own crosses to the location where they would be put to death. Thus, Christ's message was clear: in order to follow Him, Christ's disciples must deny themselves and, instead, trust Him completely. Nothing has changed since then.

If we are to be disciples of Christ, we must trust Him and place Him at the very center of our beings. Jesus never comes "next." He is always first.

Do you seek to be a worthy disciple of Christ? Then pick up His cross today and every day that you live. When you do, He will bless you now and forever.

Discipleship is a daily discipline: we follow Jesus a step at a time, a day at a time.

Warren Wiersbe

GREAT IDEAS FROM GOLFING GREATS

Golf is like chess. You have to think ahead. Plot the hole back from the flag.

Tom Watson

Play every shot so that the next one will be the easiest that you can give yourself.

Billy Casper

The object of golf is to beat someone. Make sure that someone is not yourself.

Bobby Jones

✕ A TIMELY TIP ✕

Today, think of at least one single step that you can take to become a better disciple for Christ. Then, take that step.

Work hard, but not just to please your masters when they are watching. As slaves of Christ, do the will of God with all your heart. Work with enthusiasm, as though you were working for the Lord rather than for people.

Ephesians 6:6-7 NLT

127

TOO BUSY?

Don't burn out; keep yourselves fueled and aflame. Be alert servants of the Master, cheerfully expectant. Don't quit in hard times; pray all the harder.

Romans 12:11-12 MSG

Has the hectic pace of life robbed you of the peace that might otherwise be yours through Jesus Christ? Are you one of those people who is simply too busy for your own good? If so, you're doing everybody a disservice by heaping needless stresses upon yourself and your loved ones.

God offers you a peace that passes human understanding, but He won't force His peace upon you; in order to experience it, you must slow down long enough to sense His presence and His love.

Today, as a gift to yourself, to your family, and to your world, invite Christ to preside over every aspect of your life. It's the best way to live and the surest path to peace . . . today and forever.

We often become mentally and spiritually barren because we're so busy.

Franklin Graham

IMPROVING YOUR SWING

Many times, there's nothing wrong with your swing other than bad alignment. Once your alignment is corrected, your swing falls into the groove.

Kathy Whitworth

The simpler the stroke, the more effective it will be under pressure.

Billy Casper

Many shots are spoiled at the last instant by efforts to add a few more yards.

Bobby Jones

✕ A TIMELY TIP ✕

The world wants to grab every spare minute of your time, but God wants some of your time, too. When in doubt, trust God.

Careful planning puts you ahead in the long run; hurry and scurry puts you further behind.

Proverbs 21:5 MSG

HIS PROMISES

As for God, his way is perfect. All the LORD's promises prove true. He is a shield for all who look to him for protection.

Psalm 18:30 NLT

God has made quite a few promises to you, and He will keep every single one of them.

Elisabeth Elliot observed, "We have ample evidence that the Lord is able to guide. The promises cover every imaginable situation. All we need to do is to take the hand He stretches out." And her words apply to you and to every situation you will ever encounter.

Are you facing a tough shot in the game of life? Pause for a moment and have a quiet consultation with your ultimate Advisor. Are you fearful, anxious, fretful, or troubled? Slow yourself down long enough to consider God's promises. Those promises never fail and they never grow old. You can trust those promises, and you can share them with your family, with your friends, and with the world . . . starting now . . . and ending never.

When we meditate on God and remember the promises He has given us in His Word, our faith grows, and our fears dissolve.

Charles Stanley

GREAT IDEAS FROM GOLFING GREATS

To be consistently effective, you must put a certain distance between yourself and what happens to you on the golf course.

Sam Snead

The most important thing for me in preparing for a major tournament is basic peace of mind.

Jack Nicklaus

The game isn't fair, but then life isn't fair either.

Lee Trevino

A TIMELY TIP

Today, think about the role that God's Word plays in your life, and think about ways that you can worry less and trust God more.

Patient endurance is what you need now, so you will continue to do God's will. Then you will receive all that he has promised.

Hebrews 10:36 NLT

FACING FEARS

Don't be afraid, for I am with you. Do not be dismayed for I am your God. I will strengthen you. I will help you. I will uphold you with my victorious right hand.

Isaiah 41:10 NLT

We live in a world that is, at times, a frightening place. We live in a world that is, at times, a discouraging place. We live in a world where life-changing losses can be so painful and so profound that it seems we will never recover. But, with God's help, and with the help of encouraging family members and friends, we can recover.

During the darker days of life, we are wise to remember the words of Jesus, who reassured His disciples, saying, "Take courage! It is I. Don't be afraid" (Matthew 14:27 NIV). Then, with God's comfort and His love in our hearts, we can offer encouragement to others. And by helping them face their fears, we can, in turn, tackle our own problems with courage, determination, and faith.

People who focus on their fears don't grow. They become paralyzed.

John Maxwell

PERFECTING YOUR PUTTING

Make sure your putterhead never moves outside your line during your stroke.

Lee Trevino

The putting stroke is simplest of all because it is the shortest.

Bobby Jones

The sweet spot is the area of the putter face that produces the most solid impact. Find it.

Arnold Palmer

TODAY'S SCORE CARD

Jot Down Your Thoughts About . . .
The Futility of Fear

_____

_____

_____

_____

_____

_____

THE RIGHT KIND OF FEAR

The fear of the Lord is the beginning of knowledge, but fools despise wisdom and discipline.

Proverbs 1:7 NIV

Do you have a healthy, fearful respect for God's power? If so, you are both wise and obedient. And, because you are a thoughtful believer, you also understand that genuine wisdom begins with a profound appreciation for God's limitless power.

God praises humility and punishes pride. That's why God's greatest servants will always be those humble men and women who care less for their own glory and more for God's glory. In God's kingdom, the only way to achieve greatness is to shun it. And the only way to be wise is to understand these facts: God is great; He is all-knowing; and He is all-powerful. We must respect Him, and we must humbly obey His commandments, or we must accept the consequences of our misplaced pride.

The remarkable thing about fearing God is that when you fear God, you fear nothing else, whereas if you do not fear God, you fear everything else.

Oswald Chambers

GREAT IDEAS FROM GOLFING GREATS

Try to think where you want to put the ball, not where you don't want it to go.

Billy Casper

Sometimes the biggest problem is in your head. You've got to believe you can play a shot instead of wondering where your next bad shot is coming from.

Jack Nicklaus

You can't get too keyed up about the bounces a golf ball takes.

Greg Norman

✕ A TIMELY TIP ✕

Your respect for God should make you fearful of disobeying Him . . . very fearful.

Fear the LORD your God, serve him only and take your oaths in his name.

Deuteronomy 6:13 NIV

BEYOND FAILURE

For a righteous man may fall seven times and rise again.

Proverbs 24:16 NKJV

Mary Pickford was "America's sweetheart" in the early days of motion pictures. Along with Charlie Chaplin, Douglas Fairbanks, and D.W. Griffith, she formed United Artists Corporation, a Hollywood powerhouse.

Miss Pickford had a simple yet powerful formula for success: She said, "This thing we call 'failure' is not falling down, but staying down." That's great advice for the game of life and the game of golf.

Hebrews 10:36 advises, "Patient endurance is what you need now, so you will continue to do God's will. Then you will receive all that he has promised" (NLT). These words remind us that when we persevere, we will eventually receive the rewards which God has promised us. What's required is perseverance, not perfection.

Fear is a self-imposed prison that will keep you from becoming what God intends for you to be.

Rick Warren

PERFECTING YOUR PUTTING

In standing over a putt, my first priority is comfort.

Bob Charles

The place where lack of confidence shows up with catastrophic results is most often on the greens.

Nancy Lopez

Hit the putt as well as you can, and do not worry over the outcome to ruin the stroke.

Bobby Jones

A TIMELY TIP

Time and again, the Bible preaches the power of perseverance. Setbacks, disappointments, and failures are inevitable—your response to them is optional. If you don't give up, you can turn your stumbling blocks into stepping stones.

If we confess our sins to him, he is faithful and just to forgive us and to cleanse us from every wrong.

1 John 1:9 NLT

FOCUSED ON APPEARANCES?

God does not see the same way people see. People look at the outside of a person, but the Lord looks at the heart.

1 Samuel 16:7 NCV

It's stressful to "keep up appearances." And besides, it's fruitless. After all, the world sees you as you appear to be, but God sees you as you really are—He sees your heart, and He understands your intentions. The opinions of others should be relatively unimportant to you; however, God's view of you—His understanding of your actions, your thoughts, and your motivations—should be vitally important.

Few things in life are more futile than keeping up appearances for the sake of others. What is important, of course, is pleasing your Father in heaven while you provide support and encouragement to your family members and your closest friends.

Today, do yourself a favor: worry less about physical appearances and more about spiritual realities. It's the wise way—and the peaceful way—to live.

IMPROVING YOUR SWING

The tempo experts tell us the backswing is about one-third of the downswing speed, but don't you dare think about that! Swing to waltz music and forget about thinking.

Patty Sheehan

Tension is golf's worst enemy.

Bobby Jones

No good player ever swings as hard as he can. Power is a matter of timing, not overpowering the ball.

Arnold Palmer

✕ A TIMELY TIP ✕

How you appear to other people doesn't make much difference, but how you appear to God makes all the difference.

And why worry about your clothes? Look at the lilies and how they grow. They don't work or make their clothing, yet Solomon in all his glory was not dressed as beautifully as they are.

Matthew 6:28-29 NLT

THE SIMPLE LIFE

Whoever becomes simple and elemental again, like this child, will rank high in God's kingdom.

Matthew 18:4 MSG

Asimple golf swing usually works best, and a simple life usually works best, too.

Want to reduce stress during these tough? Here's a simple solution: Simplify your life. Unfortunately, it's easier said than done. After all, you live in a world where simplicity is in short supply.

Think for a moment about the complexity of your everyday life and compare it to the lives of your ancestors. Certainly, you are the beneficiary of many technological innovations, but those innovations have a price: in all likelihood, your world is highly complex. Unless you take firm control of your time and your life, you may be overwhelmed by a stress-inducing tidal wave of complexity that threatens your happiness.

Your Heavenly Father understands the joy of living simply, and so should you. So do yourself a favor: Keep your life as simple as possible. Simplicity is, indeed, genius. By simplifying your life, you are destined to improve it.

GREAT IDEAS FROM GOLFING GREATS

The most successful way to play golf is the easiest way.

Harry Vardon

My strategy? Playing safe and within myself.

Billy Casper

If you play poorly one day, forget it. If you play poorly the next time out, review your fundamentals. If you play poorly for a third time in a row, see your professional.

Harvey Penick

TODAY'S SCORE CARD

Jot Down Your Thoughts About . . .
Something You Can Do to Simplify Your Life Today

GOD'S PROTECTION

Though I sit in darkness, the Lord will be my light.

Micah 7:8 HCSB

Have you ever faced challenges that seemed too big to handle? Have you ever faced big problems that, despite your best efforts, simply could not be solved? If so, you know how uncomfortable it is to feel helpless in the face of difficult circumstances. Thankfully, even when there's nowhere else to turn, you can turn your thoughts and prayers to God, and He will respond.

God's hand uplifts those who turn their hearts and prayers to Him. Count yourself among that number. When you do, you can live courageously and joyfully, knowing that "this too will pass"—but that God's love for you will not. And you can draw strength from the knowledge that you are a marvelous creation, loved, protected, and uplifted by the ever-present hand of God.

Whatever hallway you're in—no matter how long, how dark, or how scary—God is right there with you.

Bill Hybels

GREAT IDEAS FROM GOLFING GREATS

There's absolutely no question that golf is a game of mind over matter.

Gary Player

There is no room on the golf course for anger or self-pity.

Greg Norman

Things can always be better, but they can also be worse. Why not look on the good side?

Fuzzy Zoeller

✕ A TIMELY TIP ✕

Earthly security is an illusion. Your only real security comes from the loving heart of God. You are protected by God . . . now and always.

The Lord your God in your midst, The Mighty One, will save; He will rejoice over you with gladness, He will quiet you with His love, He will rejoice over you with singing.

Zephaniah 3:17 NKJV

DOERS OF THE WORD

But prove yourselves doers of the word, and not merely hearers.

James 1:22 NASB

The habit of putting things off until the last minute, along with its first cousin, the habit of making excuses for work that was never done, can be detrimental to your life and to your character.

Are you in the habit of doing what needs to be done when it needs to be done, or are you a dues-paying member of the Procrastinator's Club? If you've acquired the habit of doing things sooner rather than later, congratulations! But, if you find yourself putting off all those unpleasant tasks until later (or never), it's time to think about the consequences of your behavior.

One way that you can learn to defeat procrastination is by paying less attention to your fears and more attention to your responsibilities. So, when you're faced with a difficult choice or an unpleasant responsibility, don't spend endless hours fretting over your fate. Simply seek God's counsel and get busy. When you do, you will be richly rewarded because of your willingness to act.

IMPROVING YOUR SWING

Nobody ever swung a golf club too slowly.

Bobby Jones

When practicing, use the club that gives you the most trouble, not the one that gives you the most satisfaction.

Harry Vardon

Once you've grooved your swing, you shouldn't be conscious of making any fundamental changes, no matter what club you are using.

Ben Hogan

A TIMELY TIP

Today, pick out one important obligation that you've been putting off. Then, take at least one specific step toward the completion of the task you've been avoiding. Even if you don't finish the job, you'll discover that it's easier to finish a job that you've already begun than to finish a job that you've never started.

If the way you live isn't consistent with what you believe, then it's wrong.

Romans 14:23 MSG

145

WHEN OTHER PEOPLE BEHAVE BADLY

Bad temper is contagious—don't get infected.

Proverbs 22:25 MSG

Face it: sometimes people can be difficult to deal with . . . very, very difficult. When other people are unkind to you, you may be tempted to strike back, either verbally or in some other way. Resist that temptation. Instead, remember that God corrects other people's behaviors in His own way, and He doesn't need your help (even if you're totally convinced that He does).

So when other people behave cruelly, foolishly, or impulsively—as they will from time to time—don't respond in kind. Instead, speak up for yourself as politely as you can, and walk away. Then, forgive everybody as quickly as you can and leave the rest up to God.

A keen sense of humor helps us to overlook the unbecoming, understand the unconventional, tolerate the unpleasant, overcome the unexpected, and outlast the unbearable.

Billy Graham

GREAT IDEAS FROM GOLFING GREATS

The only thing that can get in the way of a golfer's success is the golfer himself.

Billy Casper

Course management is the key to golf. Somewhere along the way, you must figure out how to get the ball into the hole in the fewest shots possible.

Meg Mallon

Every shot has its own risk/reward factor.

Tom Watson

A TIMELY TIP

Don't allow yourself to become caught up in another person's emotional outbursts. If someone is ranting, raving, or worse, you have the right to get up and leave.

Real wisdom, God's wisdom, begins with a holy life and is characterized by getting along with others. It is gentle and reasonable, overflowing with mercy and blessings, not hot one day and cold the next, not two-faced.

James 3:17 MSG

147

CHARACTER MATTERS

People with integrity have firm footing, but those who follow crooked paths will slip and fall.

Proverbs 10:9 NLT

Charles Swindoll correctly observed, "Nothing speaks louder or more powerfully than a life of integrity." Thoughtful golfers agree.

Character is built slowly over a lifetime. It is the sum of every right decision, every honest word, every noble thought, and every heartfelt prayer. It is forged on the anvil of honorable work and polished by the twin virtues of generosity and humility. Character is a precious thing—difficult to build but easy to tear down. So, we must seek to live each day with discipline, honesty, and faith. When we do, integrity becomes a habit.

Whether you're on the golf course or off, you can be sure that the times that try your soul are also the times that build your character. During the darker days of life, you can learn lessons that are impossible to learn during sunny, happier days. Times of adversity can—and should—be times of intense spiritual and personal growth. But God will not force you to learn the lessons of adversity. You must learn them for yourself.

GREAT IDEAS FROM GOLFING GREATS

Golf is a game of honor. If you're playing it any other way, you're not getting the fullest satisfaction from it.

Harvey Penick

Golf is a game of integrity.

Raymond Floyd

True golfers police themselves.

Bruce Crampton

TODAY'S SCORE CARD

Jot Down Your Thoughts About . . .
The Importance of Integrity

_____

_____

_____

_____

_____

_____

_____

TODAY IS A NEW BEGINNING

You are being renewed in the spirit of your minds; you put on the new man, the one created according to God's likeness in righteousness and purity of the truth.

Ephesians 4:23-24 HCSB

Each new day offers countless opportunities to serve God, to seek His will, and to obey His teachings. But each day also offers countless opportunities to stray from God's commandments and to wander far from His path.

Sometimes, we wander aimlessly in a wilderness of our own making, but God has better plans of us. And, whenever we ask Him to renew our strength and guide our steps, He does so.

Consider this day a new beginning. Consider it a fresh start, a renewed opportunity to serve your Creator with willing hands and a loving heart. Ask God to renew your sense of purpose as He guides your steps. Today is a glorious opportunity to serve God. Seize that opportunity while you can; tomorrow may indeed be too late.

GREAT IDEAS FROM GOLFING GREATS

If you have to remind yourself to concentrate during competition, you have no chance to concentrate.

Bobby Nichols

The difference between winning and losing is always a mental one.

Peter Thomson

I'm about five inches from being an outstanding golfer. That's the distance my left ear is from my right.

Ben Crenshaw

✕ A TIMELY TIP ✕

If you're beginning a new endeavor, be sure to make God your partner. If you do, He'll guide your steps, He'll help carry your burdens, and He'll help you focus on the things that really matter.

And He who sits on the throne said, "Behold, I am making all things new."

Revelation 21:5 NASB

151

CHEERFULNESS 101

Every day is hard for those who suffer, but a happy heart is like a continual feast.

Proverbs 15:15 NCV

Cheerfulness is a wonderful asset in the game of life and the game of golf. And, as Christians, why shouldn't we be cheerful? The answer, of course, is that we have every reason to honor our Savior with joy in our hearts, smiles on our faces, and words of celebration on our lips.

Where does cheerfulness begin? It begins on the inside—in our hearts, our thoughts, and our prayers—and it works its way out from there.

The world would like you to believe that material possessions can create happiness, but don't believe it. Lasting happiness can't be bought; it must be earned— earned with positive thoughts, heartfelt prayers, good deeds, and a cheerful heart . . . like yours.

It is not fitting, when one is in God's service, to have a gloomy face or a chilling look.

St. Francis of Assisi

IMPROVING YOUR SWING

A faulty swing ties you up so that a smooth stroke becomes impossible.

Bobby Jones

My goal? Consistency. I try to do the same thing each time out.

Greg Norman

Even a flawed swing can be effective if it is repeatable.

Cary Middlecoff

A TIMELY TIP

Cheerfulness is its own reward—but not its only reward.

Be cheerful. Keep things in good repair. Keep your spirits up. Think in harmony. Be agreeable. Do all that, and the God of love and peace will be with you for sure.

2 Corinthians 13:11 MSG

WHEN OUR PLANS DON'T WORK OUT

Be strong and courageous. Do not be terrified; do not be discouraged, for the LORD your God will be with you wherever you go.

Joshua 1:9 NIV

Some of our most important dreams are the ones we abandon. Some of our most important goals are the ones we don't attain. Sometimes, our most important journeys are the ones that we take to the winding conclusion of what seem to be dead-end streets. Thankfully, with God there are no dead-ends; there are only opportunities to learn, to yield, to trust, to serve, and to grow.

The next time you experience one of life's inevitable disappointments, don't despair and don't be afraid to try "Plan B." Consider every setback an opportunity to choose a different, more appropriate path. Have faith that God may indeed be leading you in an entirely different direction, a direction of His choosing. And as you take your next step, remember that what looks like a dead-end to you may, in fact, be the fast lane according to God.

PERFECTING YOUR PUTTING

Address the putt with your eyes directly over the ball.

Gary Player

Becoming too careful, trying to be too precise, causes a golfer to freeze over his putt.

Bobby Jones

A putt cannot go in the hole if it's short. I'd rather face a four-footer coming back than leave the ball on the front lip.

Tom Watson

⚥ A TIMELY TIP ⚥

Don't spend too much time asking, "Why me, Lord?" Instead, ask, "What now, Lord?" and then get to work. When you do, you'll feel much better.

There is a time for everything, and a season for every activity under heaven.

Ecclesiastes 3:1 NIV

155

PRAISE HIM

*Praise the LORD. Give thanks to the LORD, for he is good;
his love endures forever.*

Psalm 106:1 NIV

Sometimes, in our rush to get things done, we simply don't stop long enough to pause and thank our Creator for the countless blessings He has bestowed upon us. After all, we're busy people with many demands upon our time . . . and we have so much to do. But when we slow down long enough to express our gratitude to the One who made us, we enrich our own lives and the lives of those around us.

Thanksgiving should become a habit, a regular part of our daily routines. After all, God has blessed us beyond measure, and we owe Him everything, including our constant praise.

So today, pause and count your blessings. Then, give thanks to the Giver. God's love for you is never-ending; your praise for Him should be never-ending, too.

Stand up and bless the Lord, ye people of his choice; stand up and bless the Lord your God with heart and soul and voice.

James Montgomery

GREAT IDEAS FROM GOLFING GREATS

Golf puts a man's character on the anvil and his richest qualities—patience, poise, and restraint—to the flame.

Billy Casper

If you can afford only one lesson, tell the pro you want it on the fundamentals: the grip, the stance, and the alignment.

Nancy López

When it comes time to hit, don't leap at the ball, but keep on swinging until the ball has had a good start down the fairway, and the clubhead has done its job.

Bobby Jones

TODAY'S SCORE CARD

Jot Down Your Thoughts About . . .
Important Things You're Thankful For

A SERIES OF CHOICES

The thing you should want most is God's kingdom and doing what God wants. Then all these other things you need will be given to you.

Matthew 6:33 NCV

I n every round of golf, and in every phase of life, you have choices to make. Lots of choices.

From the instant you wake up in the morning until the moment you nod off to sleep at night, you make lots of decisions: decisions about the things you do, decisions about the words you speak, and decisions about the thoughts you choose to think.

Today and every day, it's up to you (and only you) to make wise choices, choices that enhance your relationship with God. After all, He deserves no less than your best . . . and so do you.

God is voting for us all the time. The devil is voting against us all the time. The way we vote carries the election.

Corrie ten Boom

IMPROVING YOUR SWING

Lift the club with a light grip, so that it feels heavy, like using an ax. You don't hit with an ax, you accelerate it. That is exactly what you should do with a golf club.

Peter Thomson

Swing with ease against a breeze.

Golf Digest Tip

Hit against a firm left side, but hit with the right side. That's the source of power.

Calvin Peete

A TIMELY TIP

Every step of your life's journey is a choice . . . and the quality of those choices determines the quality of the journey.

Above all and before all, do this: Get Wisdom! Write this at the top of your list: Get Understanding!

Proverbs 4:7 MSG

SEEKING GOD AND FINDING HAPPINESS

But happy are those . . . whose hope is in the LORD their God.

Psalm 146:5 NLT

Happiness depends less upon our circumstances than upon our thoughts. When we turn our thoughts to God, to His gifts, and to His glorious creation, we experience the joy that God intends for His children. But, when we focus on the negative aspects of life, we inadvertently bring needless pain to our friends, to our families, and to ourselves.

Do you sincerely want to be a happy person? Then set your mind and your heart upon God's love and His grace. Seek a genuine, intimate, life-altering relationship with your Creator by studying His Word and trusting His promises. And while you're at it, count your blessings instead of your hardships. Then, after you've done these things, claim the joy, the peace, and the spiritual abundance that the Shepherd offers His sheep.

Whoever possesses God is happy.

St. Augustine

TODAY'S BIG IDEAS ABOUT GOLF AND LIFE

Enjoy the game. Happy golf is good golf.

Gary Player

God has charged Himself with full responsibility for our eternal happiness and stands ready to take over the management of our lives the moment we turn in faith to Him.

A. W. Tozer

The happiness which brings enduring worth to life is not the superficial happiness that is dependent on circumstances. It is the happiness and contentment that fills the soul in the midst of the most distressing of circumstances.

Billy Graham

✕ A TIMELY TIP ✕

Don't seek happiness. Seek God's will and live it. Happiness will follow.

Happy are those who fear the Lord. Yes, happy are those who delight in doing what he commands.

Psalm 112:1 NLT

BEYOND GUILT

There is therefore now no condemnation to those who are in Christ Jesus, who do not walk according to the flesh, but according to the Spirit.

Romans 8:1 NKJV

All of us have made mistakes. Sometimes our failures result from our own shortsightedness. On other occasions, we are swept up in events that are beyond our abilities to control. Under either set of circumstances, we may experience intense feelings of guilt. But God has an answer for the guilt that we feel. That answer, of course, is His forgiveness.

When we ask our Heavenly Father for His forgiveness, He forgives us completely and without reservation. Then, we must do the difficult work of forgiving ourselves in the same way that God has forgiven us: thoroughly and unconditionally.

If you're feeling guilty, then it's time for a special kind of housecleaning—a housecleaning of your mind and your heart . . . beginning NOW!

If God has forgiven you, why can't you forgive yourself?

Marie T. Freeman

GREAT IDEAS FROM GOLFING GREATS

Golf is not a game of great shots. It's a game of the most accurate misses.

Gene Littler

The secret of playing well is to find your comfort level, play smart, and avoid mistakes.

David Duval

It's like you're in a chess game. You're maneuvering for position.

Patty Sheehan

A TIMELY TIP

If you've asked for God's forgiveness, He has given it. But have you forgiven yourself? If not, the best moment to do so is this one.

Your beliefs about these things should be kept secret between you and God. People are happy if they can do what they think is right without feeling guilty.

Romans 14:22 NCV

163

GENUINE CONTENTMENT

The LORD gives strength to his people; the LORD blesses his people with peace.

Psalm 29:11 NIV

Everywhere we turn, or so it seems, the world promises us contentment and happiness. But the contentment that the world offers is fleeting and incomplete. Thankfully, the contentment that God offers is all encompassing and everlasting.

Happiness depends less upon our circumstances than upon our thoughts. When we turn our thoughts to God, to His gifts, and to His glorious creation, we experience the joy that God intends for His children. But, when we focus on the negative aspects of life—or when we disobey God's commandments—we cause ourselves needless suffering.

Do you sincerely want to be a contented Christian? Then set your mind and your heart upon God's love and His grace . . . and let Him take care of the rest.

Contentment is not escape from battle, but rather an abiding peace and confidence in the midst of battle.

Warren Wiersbe

GREAT IDEAS FROM GOLFING GREATS

A golf course is never quite the same from one day to the next. So you have to be able to meet the course on its terms, not your own.

Billy Casper

A player must determine the best way she can play a golf hole, not the best way someone else might play it.

Kathy Whitworth

I have seen many really good players attempt shots they should have known were impossible.

Bobby Jones

TODAY'S SCORE CARD

Jot Down Your Thoughts About . . .
What It Takes to Be Content

THE POWER OF PATIENCE

We urge you, brethren, admonish the unruly, encourage the fainthearted, help the weak, be patient with everyone.

1 Thessalonians 5:14 NASB

Most of us are impatient for success to arrive, on the golf course or not. Usually, we know what we want, and we know precisely when we want it: right now, if not sooner. But God may have other plans. And when God's plans differ from our own, we must trust in His infinite wisdom and in His infinite love.

As busy men and women living in a fast-paced world, many of us find that waiting quietly for God is difficult. Why? Because we are fallible human beings seeking to live according to our own timetables, not God's. In our better moments, we realize that patience is not only a virtue, but it is also a commandment from God.

God instructs us to be patient in all things. We must be patient with our families, our friends, and our own shortcomings. We must also be patient with our Creator as He unfolds His plan for our lives. And that's as it should be. After all, think how patient God has been with us.

TODAY'S BIG IDEAS ABOUT GOLF AND LIFE

To play well you must feel tranquil and at peace. I have never been troubled by nerves in golf because I felt I had nothing to lose and everything to gain.

Harry Vardon

As we wait on God, He helps us use the winds of adversity to soar above our problems. As the Bible says, "Those who wait on the LORD . . . shall mount up with wings like eagles."

Billy Graham

We must learn to wait. There is grace supplied to the one who waits.

Mrs. Charles E. Cowman

✕ A TIMELY TIP ✕

It takes time to become good, so be patient. The Bible promises that patience pays, and that's a promise you can depend on.

Knowing God leads to self-control. Self-control leads to patient endurance, and patient endurance leads to godliness.

2 Peter 1:6 NLT

167

GOD CAN HANDLE IT

I will lift up my eyes to the hills. From whence comes my help? My help comes from the Lord, Who made heaven and earth.

Psalm 121:1-2 NKJV

It's a promise that is made over and over again in the Bible: Whatever "it" is, God can handle it.

Life isn't always easy. Far from it! Sometimes, life can be very, very difficult, indeed. But even when the storm clouds form overhead, even during our most stressful moments, we're protected by a loving Heavenly Father.

When we're worried, God can reassure us; when we're sad, God can comfort us. When our hearts are broken, God is not just near; He is here. So we must lift our thoughts and prayers to Him. When we do, He will answer our prayers. Why? Because He is our shepherd, and He has promised to protect us now and forever.

He has transforming power. He can change the quality of our lives.

Charles Swindoll

GREAT IDEAS FROM GOLFING GREATS

On the golf course, concentrate on the present, forget the past, and don't look too far ahead.

Judy Rankin

Sometimes, thinking too much can destroy your momentum.

Tom Watson

Stay in the present tense.

Tom Kite

⚔ A TIMELY TIP ⚔

God isn't far away—He's right here, right now. And He's willing to talk to you right here, right now.

The LORD is my strength and song, and He has become my salvation; He is my God, and I will praise Him…

Exodus 15:2 NKJV

169

TRUSTING GOD

It is better to trust the Lord than to put confidence in people.
It is better to trust the Lord than to put confidence in princes.

Psalm 118:8-9 NLT

Sometimes the future seems bright, and sometimes it does not. Yet even when we cannot see the possibilities of tomorrow, God can. Our challenge is to trust an uncertain future to an all-powerful God.

When we trust God, we should trust Him without reservation. We should steel ourselves against the inevitable stresses of the day, secure in the knowledge that our Heavenly Father has a plan for the future that only He can see.

Can you place your future into the hands of a loving and all-knowing God? Can you live amid the uncertainties of today, knowing that God has dominion over all your tomorrows? If you can, you are wise and you are blessed. When you trust God with everything you are and everything you have, He will bless you now and forever.

God is God. He knows what he is doing. When you can't trace his hand, trust his heart.

Max Lucado

GREAT IDEAS FROM GOLFING GREATS

Fight tautness whenever it occurs; strive for relaxed muscles throughout.

Bobby Jones

The guy who believes in happy endings is going to play consistently better golf than the man who approaches every act of existence with fear and foreboding.

Tony Lema

The most important shot in golf is the next one.

Ben Hogan

⚔ A TIMELY TIP ⚔

When life seems unfair, try spending more time trusting God and less time dwelling on "the unfairness of it all."

For the Lord God is our light and our protector. He gives us grace and glory. No good thing will the Lord withhold from those who do what is right. O Lord Almighty, happy are those who trust in you.

Psalm 84:11-12 NLT

171

FINDING PEACE IN GOD'S WORD

For the word of God is quick, and powerful, and sharper than any two-edged sword, piercing even to the dividing asunder of soul and spirit, and of the joints and marrow, and is a discerner of the thoughts and intents of the heart.

Hebrews 4:12 KJV

The words of Matthew 4:4 remind us that, "Man shall not live by bread alone but by every word that proceedeth out of the mouth of God" (KJV). As Christians, we must study the Bible and meditate upon its meaning for our lives. Otherwise, we deprive ourselves of a priceless gift from our Creator.

God's Word is unlike any other book. The Bible is a roadmap for life here on earth and for life eternal. As Christians, we are called upon to study God's Holy Word, to follow its commandments, and to share its Good News with the world.

Jonathan Edwards advised, "Be assiduous in reading the Holy Scriptures. This is the fountain whence all knowledge in divinity must be derived. Therefore let not this treasure lie by you neglected." God's Word is, indeed, a priceless treasure, and a passing acquaintance with the Bible is insufficient for Christians who seek to obey God's Word and to understand His will.

GREAT IDEAS FROM GOLFING GREATS

I've learned to slap down any errant thoughts that intrude on my mind. Kick 'em off the premises and replace them with thoughts only related to the shot at hand.

Patty Sheehan

If you're serious about improving your play, be brutally honest with yourself.

Greg Norman

Concentration is a fine antidote to anxiety.

Jack Nicklaus

⨉ A TIMELY TIP ⨉

On your bookshelf you have God's roadmap for life here on earth and for life eternal. How you choose to use your Bible is, of course, up to you . . . and so are the consequences.

Blessed are those who hunger and thirst for righteousness, for they will be filled.

Matthew 5:6 NIV

A RENEWED SENSE OF PURPOSE

You will show me the path of life; in Your presence is fullness of joy; at Your right hand are pleasures forevermore.

Psalm 16:11 NKJV

God has a plan for the universe, and He has a plan for you. He understands that plan as thoroughly and completely as He knows you. If you seek God's will earnestly and prayerfully, He will make His plans known to you in His own way.

Perhaps your vision of God's purpose for your life has been clouded by a wish list that you have expected God to dutifully fulfill. Perhaps, you have fervently hoped that God would create a world that unfolds according to your wishes, not His. If so, you have probably experienced more disappointment than satisfaction and more frustration than peace. A better strategy is to conform your will to God's (and not to struggle vainly in an attempt to conform His will to yours).

Sometimes, God's plans and purposes may seem unmistakably clear to you. If so, push ahead. But other times, He may lead you through the wilderness before He directs you to the Promised Land. So be patient and keep seeking His will for your life. When you do, you'll be amazed at the marvelous things that God can do.

PERFECTING YOUR PUTTING

The man who says his knees aren't shaking as he stands over a this-to-win putt is lying.

Ian Woosnam

Keep the stroke as simple as possible.

Gay Brewer

The less said about the putter, the better. Here is an element of torture.

Tony Lema

⨯ A TIMELY TIP ⨯

Ten years from now you will be somewhere—the question is where? You and God, working together, will shape your future. And remember: it's not about earning a living; it's about designing a life.

Whatever you do, do all to the glory of God.

1 Corinthians 10:31 NKJV

175

RELY UPON HIM

Therefore humble yourselves under the mighty hand of God, that He may exalt you at the proper time, casting all your anxiety on Him, because He cares for you.

1 Peter 5:6-7 NASB

Do the stresses of these turbulent times threaten to overwhelm you? If so, you must rely not only upon your own resources but also upon the promises of your Father in heaven.

God is a never-ending source of support and courage for those of us who call upon Him. When we are weary, He gives us strength. When we see no hope, God reminds us of His promises. When we grieve, God wipes away our tears.

God will hold your hand and walk with you every day of your life if you let Him. So even if your circumstances are difficult, trust the Father. His love is eternal and His goodness endures forever.

God is bigger than your problems. Whatever worries press upon you today, put them in God's hands and leave them there.

Billy Graham

GREAT IDEAS FROM GOLFING GREATS

I believe most sincerely that the impulse to steer, born of anxiety, is accountable for almost every really bad shot.

Bobby Jones

Nervous tension is the biggest enemy in golf.

Sandra Haynie

Remember—you have to be comfortable. Golf is not a life or death situation. It's just a game and should be treated as such. Stay loose.

Chi Chi Rodriguez

✕ A TIMELY TIP ✕

God wants to provide for you and your loved ones. When you trust your life and your future to God, He will provide for your needs.

Finally, my brethren, be strong in the Lord and in the power of His might. Put on the whole armor of God, that you may be able to stand against the wiles of the devil.

Ephesians 6:10-11 NKJV

DAY 85

COUNTING YOUR BLESSINGS

Blessings crown the head of the righteous....

Proverbs 10:6 NIV

Because we have been so richly blessed, we should make thanksgiving a habit, a regular part of our daily routines. But sometimes, amid the stresses and obligations of everyday life, we may allow interruptions and distractions to interfere with the time we spend with God.

Have you counted your blessings today? And have you thanked God for them? Hopefully so. After all, God's gifts include your family, your friends, your talents, your opportunities, your possessions, and the priceless gift of eternal life. How glorious are these gifts . . . and God is responsible for every one of them.

So today, as you go about the duties of everyday life, pause and give thanks to the Creator. He deserves your praise, and you deserve the experience of praising Him.

God is more anxious to bestow His blessings on us than we are to receive them.

St. Augustine

IMPROVING YOUR SWING

Make up your mind before your backswing starts, then let your muscles do the work.

Tommy Armour

I want to make this game easy. Improving my swing is a simplifying principle. It eliminates a lot of clutter, a lot of false issues.

Tom Watson

Hum your favorite waltz and swing to the beat of the tune.

Sam Snead

TODAY'S SCORE CARD

Jot Down Your Thoughts About . . .
The Blessings That God Has Given You

_____

_____

_____

_____

_____

_____

THE LESSONS OF TOUGH TIMES

If you hide your sins, you will not succeed. If you confess and reject them, you will receive mercy.

Proverbs 28:13 NCV

Have you experienced a recent setback on the golf course or off? If so, look for the lesson that God is trying to teach you. Instead of complaining about life's sad state of affairs, learn what needs to be learned, change what needs to be changed, and move on. View failure as an opportunity to reassess God's will for your life. And while you're at it, consider life's inevitable disappointments to be powerful opportunities to learn more—more about yourself, more about your circumstances, and more about your world.

Life can be difficult at times. And everybody (including you) makes mistakes. Your job is to make them only once. And how can you do that? By learning the lessons of tough times sooner rather than later, that's how.

Measure the size of the obstacles against the size of God.

Beth Moore

TODAY'S BIG IDEAS ABOUT GOLF AND LIFE

Golf is a game of mistakes. The best players make the smallest mistakes.

Sam Snead

Father, take our mistakes and turn them into opportunities.

Max Lucado

There are only two kinds of problems: the ones that are small enough for you to handle, and the ones that aren't too big for God to handle.

Criswell Freeman

✕ A TIMELY TIP ✕

On the golf course, the fear of failure is your enemy. So, don't be afraid of making mistakes. And, when you make a bad shot, put it behind you before you take your next swing.

———————

God is our refuge and strength, a very present help in trouble.

Psalm 46:1 NKJV

THE QUIET GAME

In quietness and trust is your strength.

Isaiah 30:15 NASB

The world seems to grow louder day by day, and our senses seem to be invaded at every turn. If we allow the distractions of a clamorous society to separate us from God's peace, we do ourselves a profound disservice. Our task, as dutiful believers, is to carve out moments of silence in a world filled with noise. Golf is intended to be a quiet game; perhaps that's one of its greatest allures.

Has the busy pace of life robbed you of the peace that God has promised? If so, it's time to reorder your priorities and your life. Nothing is more important than the quiet time you spend with your Heavenly Father. So be still and claim the inner peace that is found in the silent moments you spend with God.

A quiet time is a basic ingredient in a maturing relationship with God.

Charles Stanley

PERFECTING YOUR PUTTING

You have to be a good putter to be a good golfer, but you don't necessarily have to be a good golfer to be a good putter.

Tony Lema

You live by the putter, and you die by the putter.

Old Golf Saying

You work all your life to perfect a repeating swing that will get you to the greens, and then you have to try to do something that is totally unrelated: putting. There shouldn't be any cups, just flag sticks. And then the man who hits the most fairways and greens and gets closest to the pins would be the tournament winner.

Ben Hogan

✕ A TIMELY TIP ✕

In golf, as in life, silence is beautiful. Today, find time to be still and listen to God. He has something important to say to you.

Be still before the Lord and wait patiently for Him.

Psalm 37:7 NIV

DAY 88

CRITICS BEWARE

Don't criticize one another, brothers. He who criticizes a brother or judges his brother criticizes the law and judges the law. But if you judge the law, you are not a doer of the law but a judge.

James 4:11 HCSB

From experience, we know that it is easy to criticize others. And we know that it is usually far easier to find faults than to find solutions. Still, the urge to criticize others remains a powerful temptation for most of us.

Negativity is highly contagious: We give it to others who, in turn, give it back to us. This stress-inducing cycle can be broken only by positive thoughts, heartfelt prayers, encouraging words, and meaningful acts of kindness.

As thoughtful servants of a loving God, we have no valid reason—and no legitimate excuse—to be negative. So, when we are tempted to be overly critical of others, or unfairly critical of ourselves, we must use the transforming power of God's love to break the chains of negativity. We must defeat negativity before negativity defeats us.

184

GREAT IDEAS FROM GOLFING GREATS

Golfers have analyzed the game in order to find "the secret." There is no secret.

Henry Cotton

It's just as important to sink a bogey putt as it is to drop one for a par.

Doug Ford

Make the hard ones look easy and the easy ones look hard.

Walter Hagen

⨯ A TIMELY TIP ⨯

If you're too critical of other people—or of yourself—it's time to become more forgiving and less judgmental.

Let angry people endure the backlash of their own anger; if you try to make it better, you'll only make it worse.

Proverbs 19:19 MSG

YOUR OWN WORST CRITIC?

My dear children, let's not just talk about love; let's practice real love. This is the only way we'll know we're living truly, living in God's reality. It's also the way to shut down debilitating self-criticism, even when there is something to it. For God is greater than our worried hearts and knows more about us than we do ourselves. And friends, once that's taken care of and we're no longer accusing or condemning ourselves, we're bold and free before God!

1 John 3:18-21 MSG

Are you your own worst critic on the links or off? If so, it's time to become a little more understanding of the person you see whenever you look into the mirror.

Being patient with other people can be difficult. But sometimes, we find it even more difficult to be patient with ourselves. We have high expectations and lofty goals. We want to receive God's blessings now, not later. And, of course, we want our lives to unfold according to our own wishes and our own timetables—not God's. Yet throughout the Bible, we are instructed that patience is the companion of wisdom. Proverbs 16:32 teaches us that "Patience is better than strength" (NCV). God's message is clear: we must be patient with all people.

The Bible affirms the importance of self-acceptance by exhorting believers to love others as they love them-selves (Matthew 22:37-40). Furthermore, the Bible teaches that when we genuinely open our hearts to Him, God accepts us just as we are. And, if He accepts us—faults and all—then who are we to believe otherwise?

GREAT IDEAS FROM GOLFING GREATS

More than any other game, golf is about self-control, restraint of personality, and the mastering of the emotions.

Thomas Boswell

My reaction to anything that happens on the golf course is no reaction. There are no birdies or bogeys, no eagles or double bogeys; there are only numbers. If you can learn that, you can play this game.

Jim Colbert

Never let emotions interfere with the ability to make smart decisions.

Curtis Strange

FINDING PEACE

These things I have spoken to you, that in Me you may have peace. In the world you will have tribulation; but be of good cheer, I have overcome the world.

John 16:33 NKJV

A golf course should be a peaceful place, but sometimes players allow themselves to become frustrated, discouraged, or angry. Oftentimes, our outer struggles are simply manifestations of the inner conflict we feel when we stray from God's path. Jesus offers us peace, not as the world gives, but as He alone gives. Our challenge is to accept Christ's peace into our hearts and then, as best we can, to share His peace with our neighbors. When we accept Jesus as our personal Savior, we are transformed by His grace. We are then free to accept the spiritual abundance and peace that can be ours through the power of the risen Christ.

Today, claim the inner peace that is your spiritual birthright: the peace of Jesus Christ. It is offered freely; it has been paid for in full; it is yours for the asking. So ask. And then share.

Before God changes our circumstances, He wants to change our hearts.

Warren Wiersbe

GREAT IDEAS FROM GOLFING GREATS

Golf is a game of precision, not strength.

Jack Nicklaus

Golf is a great and glorious game. Even those of us who earn our livings at it play it more for the pleasure than for the money.

Arnold Palmer

Golf is like eating peanuts. You can play too much or play too little.

Bobby Jones

✕ A TIMELY TIP ✕

God's peace surpasses human understanding. When you accept His peace, it will revolutionize your life.

God has called us to peace.

1 Corinthians 7:15 NKJV

189

TEMPTATIONS EVERYWHERE

No temptation has seized you except what is common to man. And God is faithful; he will not let you be tempted beyond what you can bear. But when you are tempted, he will also provide a way out so that you can stand up under it.

1 Corinthians 10:13 NIV

If you stop to think about it, the cold, hard evidence is right in front of your eyes: you live in a temptation-filled world. The devil is out on the street, hard at work, causing pain, stress, and heartache in more ways than ever before. Here in the 21st century, the bad guys are working around the clock to lead you astray. That's why you must remain vigilant.

In a letter to believers, Peter offered a stern warning: "Your adversary, the devil, prowls around like a roaring lion, seeking someone to devour" (1 Peter 5:8 NASB). What was true in New Testament times is equally true in our own. Satan tempts his prey and then devours them. So, we must beware: If we wish to live wisely and well, we must earnestly wrap ourselves in the protection of God's Holy Word. When we do, we are secure.

TODAY'S BIG IDEAS ABOUT GOLF AND LIFE

Play within yourself—play your own game.

Billy Casper

The scoring at golf is as much about avoiding disasters as making birdies.

Jack Nicklaus

We have both help to endure temptation and pardon when we fall into it—we have every remedy for sin. We have Jesus.

Franklin Graham

TODAY'S SCORE CARD

Jot Down Your Thoughts About . . .
Temptations You Should Resist Today

USING YOUR TALENTS

Do not neglect the gift that is in you.

1 Timothy 4:14 NKJV

God gives each of us a unique assortment of talents and opportunities. And our Heavenly Father instructs us to be faithful stewards of the gifts that He bestows upon us. But we live in a world that encourages us to do otherwise.

Ours is a society that is filled to the brim with countless opportunities to squander our time, our resources, and our talents. So we must be watchful for distractions and temptations that might lead us astray.

God has blessed you with unique opportunities to serve Him, and He has given you every tool that you need to do so. Today, accept this challenge: value the talent that God has given you, nourish it, make it grow, and share it with the world. After all, the best way to say "Thank You" for God's gifts is to use them.

God often reveals His direction for our lives through the way He made us, with a certain personality and unique skills.

Bill Hybels

GREAT IDEAS FROM GOLFING GREATS

Give it your best, but always with the realization that your happiness and your livelihood are not riding on the next shot.

Jane Blalock

You never master golf. You take what it gives, and you learn from it.

Charlie Sifford

Don't be in such a hurry. That little white ball isn't going to run away from you.

Patty Berg

⨯ A TIMELY TIP ⨯

God has given you a unique array of talents and opportunities. The rest is up to you.

Each man has his own gift from God; one has this gift, another has that.

1 Corinthians 7:7 NIV

193

SHARING YOUR BURDENS WITH GOD

If God is for us, who can be against us?

Romans 8:31 NKJV

The Bible promises this: tough times are temporary but God's love is not—God's love endures forever. So what does that mean to you? Just this: From time to time, everybody faces hardships and disappointments, and so will you. And when tough times arrive, God always stands ready to protect you and to heal you. Your task is straightforward: you must share your burdens with Him.

As Corrie ten Boom observed, "Any concern that is too small to be turned into a prayer is too small to be made into a burden." Those are comforting words, especially in these difficult days.

Whatever the size of your challenges, God is big enough to handle them. Ask for His help today, with faith and with fervor. Instead of turning things over in your mind, turn them over to God in prayer. Instead of worrying about your next decision, ask God to lead the way. Cast your burdens upon the One who cannot be shaken, and rest assured that He always hears your prayers.

IMPROVING YOUR SWING

The best swing is the one that repeats.

Lee Trevino

The busier you keep yourself with the details of a particular shot, the less time your mind has to dwell on the emotional "ifs" and "buts."

Jack Nicklaus

Thinking about smooth tempo helps me maintain consistency from day to day. The major benefit of good rhythm is that it makes it easier to control distance with each club.

Annika Sorenstam

A TIMELY TIP

Earthly security is an illusion. Your only real security comes from the loving heart of God.

For the LORD your God is a merciful God....

Deuteronomy 4:31 NIV

FOCUS AND CONCENTRATION

Look straight ahead, and fix your eyes on what lies before you. Mark out a straight path for your feet; then stick to the path and stay safe. Don't get sidetracked; keep your feet from following evil.

Proverbs 4:25-27 NLT

Great golfers have the ability to focus. And, so do great Christians. What is your focus today? Are you willing to focus your thoughts and energies on God's blessings and upon His will for your life? Or will you turn your thoughts to other things? Before you answer that question, consider this: God created you in His own image, and He wants you to experience joy and abundance. But, God will not force His joy upon you; you must claim it for yourself.

Today, why not focus your thoughts on the joy that is rightfully yours in Christ? Why not take time to celebrate God's glorious creation? Why not trust your hopes instead of your fears? When you do, you will think optimistically about yourself and your world . . . and you can then share your optimism with others. They'll be better for it, and so will you. But not necessarily in that order.

GREAT IDEAS FROM GOLFING GREATS

The brain controls the mind. The mind controls the body. The body controls the club.

Mike Hebron

The difference between an ordinary player and a champion is in the way they think.

Patty Berg

Never let one bad shot disrupt your rhythm or concentration.

Sam Snead

TODAY'S SCORE CARD

Jot Down Your Thoughts About . . .
The Rewards of Focusing Your Thoughts and Energy

YOUR REAL RICHES

Don't collect for yourselves treasures on earth, where moth and rust destroy and where thieves break in and steal. But collect for yourselves treasures in heaven, where neither moth nor rust destroys, and where thieves don't break in and steal. For where your treasure is, there your heart will be also.

Matthew 6:19-21 HCSB

All too often we focus our thoughts and energies on the accumulation of earthly treasures, creating untold stress in our lives and leaving precious little time to accumulate the only treasures that really matter: the spiritual kind. Our material possessions have the potential to do great good—depending upon how we use them. If we allow the things we own to own us, we may pay dearly for our misplaced priorities.

Society focuses intently on material possessions, but God's Word teaches us time and again that money matters little when compared to the spiritual gifts that the Creator offers to those who put Him first in their lives. So today, keep your possessions in perspective. Remember that God should come first, and everything else next. When you give God His rightful place in your heart, you'll have a clearer vision of the things that really matter. Then, you can joyfully thank your heavenly Father for spiritual blessings that are, in truth, too numerous to count.

TODAY'S BIG IDEAS ABOUT GOLF AND LIFE

Every day you miss playing or practicing is one day longer it takes to be good.

Ben Hogan

What we possess often possesses us—we are possessed by possessions.

Oswald Chambers

Greed is evil because it substitutes material things for the place of honor that the Creator ought to have in an individual's life.

Charles Stanley

✕ A TIMELY TIP ✕

We all need the basic necessities of life, but once we meet those needs for ourselves and for our families, the piling up of possessions can create more problems than it solves. Our real riches, of course, are not of this world. We are never really rich until we are rich in spirit.

A pretentious, showy life is an empty life; a plain and simple life is a full life.

Proverbs 13:7 MSG

MAKE PEACE
WITH THE PAST

There is one thing I always do. Forgetting the past and straining toward what is ahead, I keep trying to reach the goal and get the prize for which God called me . . . .

Philippians 3:13–14 NCV

Because you are human, you may be slow to forget yesterday's disappointments. But, if you sincerely seek to focus your hopes and energies on the future, then you must find ways to accept the past, no matter how difficult it may be to do so.

Have you made peace with your past? If so, congratulations. But, if you are mired in the quicksand of regret, it's time to plan your escape. How can you do so? By accepting what has been and by trusting God for what will be.

So, if you have not yet made peace with the past, today is the day to declare an end to all hostilities. When you do, you can then turn your thoughts to the wondrous promises of God and to the glorious future that He has in store for you.

Don't let yesterday use up too much of today.

Dennis Swanberg

TODAY'S BIG IDEAS ABOUT GOLF AND LIFE

Every golfer can expect to have four bad shots a round. When you do, just put them out of your mind.

Walter Hagen

God forgets the past. Imitate him.

Max Lucado

Don't waste today's time cluttering up tomorrow's opportunities with yesterday's troubles.

Barbara Johnson

✕ A TIMELY TIP ✕

The past is past, so don't invest all your energy there. If you're focused on the past, change your focus. If you're living in the past, move on.

Do not remember the past events, pay no attention to things of old. Look, I am about to do something new; even now it is coming. Do you not see it? Indeed, I will make a way in the wilderness, rivers in the desert.

Isaiah 43:18-19 HCSB

201

OVER-COMMITTED?

Don't burn out; keep yourselves fueled and aflame. Be alert servants of the Master, cheerfully expectant. Don't quit in hard times; pray all the harder.

Romans 12:11-12 MSG

Do you have too many things on your to-do list and too few hours in which to do them? If so, it's time to take a long, hard look at the way you're prioritizing your days and your life.

The world encourages you to rush full-speed ahead, taking on lots of new commitments, doing many things, but doing few things well. God, on the other hand, encourages you to slow down, to quiet yourself, and to spend time with Him. And you can be sure that God's way is best.

How will you organize your life? Will you carve out quiet moments with the Creator? And while you're at it, will you focus your energies and your resources on only the most important tasks on your to-do list? Or will you max out your schedule, leaving much of your most important work undone?

Today, slow yourself down and commit more time to God. When you do, you'll be amazed at how the Father can revolutionize your life when you start spending more time with Him.

GREAT IDEAS FROM GOLFING GREATS

As long as your swing works, use it. When it stops working, change.

Lee Trevino to 12-year-old Nancy Lopez

Before you can become proficient off the tee, you have a difficult task: Remove any thought of distance. Your main objective off the tee is control.

Kathy Whitworth

Don't hit the ball. Swing at it. Develop a nice, graceful swing.

Babe Didrikson Zaharias

TODAY'S SCORE CARD

Jot Down Your Thoughts About . . .
The Personal Cost of Over-commitment

DECISIONS MATTER

If you need wisdom—if you want to know what God wants you to do—ask him, and he will gladly tell you. He will not resent your asking.

James 1:5 NLT

Life presents each of us with countless questions, conundrums, doubts, and problems. Thankfully, the riddles of everyday living are not too difficult to solve if we look for answers in the right places. When we have questions, we should consult God's Word, we should consult our own consciences, and we should consult a few close friends and family members.

Søren Kierkegaard could have been talking about life on the links when he observed, "Life can only be understood backwards; but it must be lived forwards." Taking a forward-looking (and stress-reducing) approach to life means learning the art of solving difficult problems sensibly and consistently . . . and sooner rather than later.

Every day, I find countless opportunities to decide whether I will obey God and demonstrate my love for Him or try to please myself or the world system. God is waiting for my choices.

Bill Bright

GREAT IDEAS FROM GOLFING GREATS

The best strategic advice is this: Know your strengths and take advantage of them.

Greg Norman

Every shot counts. The three-foot putt is just as important as the 300-yard drive.

Henry Cotton

On every hole, never tee it up without a plan.

Julius Boros

✕ A TIMELY TIP ✕

When you're about to make an important decision, take your time and talk to your Creator.

The thing you should want most is God's kingdom and doing what God wants. Then all these other things you need will be given to you.

Matthew 6:33 NCV

TAKING CARE OF YOUR BODY

Do you not know that your bodies are temples of the Holy Spirit, who is in you, whom you have received from God? You are not your own.

1 Corinthians 6:19 NIV

Are you concerned about your spiritual, physical, or emotional health? If so, there is a timeless source of comfort and advice that is as near as your bookshelf. That source is the Holy Bible.

God's Word has much to say about every aspect of your life, including your health. If you face personal health challenges that seem almost insoluble, have faith and seek God's wisdom. If you can't seem to get yourself on a sensible diet or on a program of regular physical exercise, consult God's teachings. If your approach to your physical or emotional health has, up to this point, been undisciplined, pray to your Creator for the strength to do what you know is right.

God has given you the Holy Bible for the purpose of knowing His promises, His power, His commandments, His wisdom, His love, and His Son. As you seek to improve the state of your own health, study God's teachings and apply them to your life. When you do, you will be blessed, now and forever.

TODAY'S BIG IDEAS ABOUT GOLF AND LIFE

One of the worst mistakes you can make in golf is trying to force the game.

Jack Nicklaus

There's no rule in golf that states "thou shall shoot for the flagstick."

Patty Sheehan

Too much ambition is a bad thing to have in a bunker.

Bobby Jones

✕ A TIMELY TIP ✕

God has given you a body, and He's placed you in charge of caring for it. Your body is a temple that should be treated with respect.

Beloved, I pray that in all respects you may prosper and be in good health, just as your soul prospers.

3 John 1:2 NASB

LET JESUS GUIDE THE WAY

I have come as a light into the world, that whoever believes in Me should not abide in darkness.

John 12:46 NKJV

The 19th-century writer Hannah Whitall Smith observed, "The crucial question for each of us is this: What do you think of Jesus, and do you yet have a personal acquaintance with Him?" Indeed, the answer to that question determines the quality, the course, and the direction of our lives today and for all eternity.

The old familiar hymn begins, "What a friend we have in Jesus . . . ." No truer words were ever penned. Jesus is the sovereign Friend and ultimate Savior of mankind. Christ showed enduring love for His believers by willingly sacrificing His own life so that we might have eternal life. Now, it is our turn to become His friend.

Let us love our Savior, praise Him, and share His message of salvation with our neighbors and with the world. When we do, we demonstrate that our acquaintance with the Master is not a passing fancy; it is, instead, the cornerstone and the touchstone of our lives.

TODAY'S BIG IDEAS ABOUT GOLF AND LIFE

Never think about what you did wrong on the last shot. Think about what you will do right on the next one.

Tommy Armour

Imagination is the death of a low golf score if you visualize hazards that don't exist.

Gene Sarazen

My father told me, "You must never learn to think the negative."

Johnny Miller

✕ A TIMELY TIP ✕

Jesus is the light of the world. Make sure that you are capturing and reflecting His light.

And Jesus said to them, "I am the bread of life. He who comes to Me shall never hunger, and he who believes in Me shall never thirst."

John 6:35 NKJV

MOVE ON

Get rid of all bitterness, rage, anger, harsh words, and slander, as well as all types of malicious behavior. Instead, be kind to each other, tenderhearted, forgiving one another, just as God through Christ has forgiven you.

Ephesians 4:31–32 NLT

The golf course holds few, if any, rewards for those who remain angrily focused upon the past. Those who are focused on the last shot seldom make the most of the next one.

Are you mired in the quicksand of bitterness or regret? If so, you are not only disobeying God's Word, you are also wasting your time.

Being frail, fallible, imperfect human beings, most of us are quick to anger, quick to blame, slow to forgive, and even slower to forget.

If there exists even one person—alive or dead—against whom you hold bitter feelings, it's time to forgive. Or, if you are embittered against yourself for some past mistake or shortcoming, it's finally time to forgive yourself and move on. Hatred, bitterness, and regret are not part of God's plan for your life. Forgiveness is.

IMPROVING YOUR SWING

Every good golfer possesses a carefully developed set of key swing thoughts that he uses to keep his game in balance.

Jack Nicklaus

The length of a drive depends not upon brute force, but upon the speed of the clubhead.

Bobby Jones

You must keep the golf swing as simple as you can. That is why I'm so adamant about fundamentals.

Kathy Whitworth

TODAY'S SCORE CARD

Jot Down Your Thoughts About . . .
The Cost of Focusing on the Past

_____

_____

_____

_____

_____

DAY 102

PREPARATION PAYS

So prepare your minds for service and have self-control.

1 Peter 1:13 NCV

In golf, as in life, practice pays. Sam Sneed said, "The only way to build realistic confidence in yourself is through practice." And Jack Nicklaus advised, "Don't be too proud to take lessons. I'm not."

The old adage is both familiar and true: We must pray as if everything depended upon God, but work as if everything depended upon us. Yet sometimes, when we are weary and discouraged, we may allow our worries to sap our energy and our hope. God has other intentions. God intends that we pray for things, and He intends that we be willing to work for the things that we pray for.

In looking back on his youth, Ben Hogan observed, "It was a great joy to improve. There wasn't enough daylight in the day for me. I always wished the days were longer so I could practice and work." And if you'd like to improve your game, get to work now because, as we read in John 9:4, "Night is coming, when no one can work."

The higher the ideal, the more work is required to accomplish it. Do not expect to become a great success in life if you are not willing to work for it.

Father Flanagan

GREAT IDEAS FROM GOLFING GREATS

You must work very hard to become a natural golfer.

Gary Player

You build a good golf game like you build a wall: one brick at a time.

Tony Lema

Don't be too anxious to see good results on the scoreboard until you've fully absorbed the principles of the golf swing on the practice tee.

Louise Suggs

TODAY'S SCORE CARD

Jot Down Your Thoughts About . . .
Ways to Improve Yourself and Your Game

DAY 103

THE GAME OF LIFE

I urge you now to live the life to which God called you.

Ephesians 4:1 NKJV

L ife should never be taken for granted. Each day is a priceless gift from God and should be treated as such. Yet at times, because we are busy people with too many obligations and too little time to complete them, we may not slow down long enough to thank the Giver of all things good. When we allow ourselves to become too busy, or too preoccupied, to praise God, we do ourselves and our loved ones a disservice.

Today, as the sun peaks over the horizon, you have yet another reason to celebrate life. Will you treat this day as a priceless treasure, a unique opportunity to follow God and celebrate His creation? You should. After all, this is God's day, and He has given us clear instructions for its use. We are commanded to rejoice and be glad. So, with no further ado, let the celebration begin.

Life is a gift from God, and we must treasure it, protect it, and invest it.

Warren Wiersbe

GREAT IDEAS FROM GOLFING GREATS

I still believe winning is 90 mental. You can swing a golf club as pretty as anyone, but if you can't visualize making the shot and believe you can make it, you can't win.

Nancy Lopez

Golf is a lot like life. It will test your patience. It will dazzle and baffle you with highs and lows, successes and frustrations. Just when you think you've got it all figured out, the game jumps up and reminds you that nobody ever quite gets it.

Amy Alcott

A TIMELY TIP

Whether you're on the course or off, every day is a priceless gift from God. How you use that gift is up to you.

Make it your ambition to lead a quiet life, to mind your own business and to work with your hands, just as we told you, so that your daily life may win the respect of outsiders and so that you will not be dependent on anybody.

1 Thessalonians 4:11-12 NIV

LEARNING TO SAY NO

So let us run the race that is before us and never give up. We should remove from our lives anything that would get in the way and the sin that so easily holds us back.

Hebrews 12:1 NCV

If you haven't yet learned to say "No"—to say it politely, firmly, and often—you're inviting untold stress into your life. Why? Because if you can't say "No" (when appropriate) to family members, friends, or coworkers, you'll find yourself overcommitted and underappreciated.

If you have trouble standing up for yourself, perhaps you're afraid that you'll be rejected. But here's a tip: don't worry too much about rejection, especially when you're rejected for doing the right thing.

Pleasing other people is a good thing . . . up to a point. But you must never allow your "willingness to please" to interfere with your own good judgment or with God's priorities.

God gave you a conscience for a reason: to inform you about the things you need to do as well as the things you don't need to do. It's up to you to follow your conscience wherever it may lead, even if it means making unpopular decisions. Your job, should you choose to accept it, is to be popular with God, not people.

GREAT IDEAS FROM GOLFING GREATS

The toughest opponent of all is Old Man Par. He's a patient soul who never shoots a birdie and never incurs a bogey. He's a patient soul, Old Man Par. And if you would travel the long road with him, you must be patient, too.

Bobby Jones

The sweetest two words are "next time." The sourest word is "if."

Chi Chi Rodriguez

✕ A TIMELY TIP ✕

Never take on a major obligation of any kind without first taking sufficient time to carefully consider whether or not you should commit to it. The bigger the obligation, the more days you should take to decide. If someone presses you for an answer before you are ready, your automatic answer should always be "No."

So teach us to number our days, that we may gain a heart of wisdom.

Psalm 90:12 NKJV

217

TROUBLES ARE TEMPORARY

We also have joy with our troubles, because we know that these troubles produce patience. And patience produces character, and character produces hope.

Romans 5:3-4 NCV

After a particularly poor round at Walton Heath, Valentine Viscount Castlerosse instructed his caddie, "Have the clubs destroyed, and leave the course." Every golfer knows the feeling. As Thomas Boswell observed, "The game of golf was created with humiliation in mind."

Because the game of golf is an exercise in humility, it is wonderful training for life. The thoughtful golfer comes to understand that hazards and bad bounces are simply part of the game. The best thing we can do about our tough breaks is to face them with determined acceptance. And play them where they lie.

Life is often challenging, but we should not be afraid. Our Father loves us, and He will protect us. In times of hardship, He will comfort us. When we are troubled, or weak, or sorrowful, God is always with us. We must build our lives on the rock that cannot be shaken . . . we must trust in God. Always.

GREAT IDEAS FROM GOLFING GREATS

The mark of a great player is in his ability to come back. The great champions have all come back from defeat.

Sam Snead

Recovering from a bad hole can be the difference between success and failure.

Gay Brewer

As I get older, I try to think of the bad things that happen to me on the golf course as "tests." They're not hurdles; they're not bad marks or punishments. They're things I need in my life, things that bring me back to reality.

Frank Beard

TODAY'S SCORE CARD

Jot Down Your Thoughts About . . .
God's Protection

BE THANKFUL

As you therefore have received Christ Jesus the Lord, so walk in Him, having been firmly rooted and now being built up in Him and established in your faith, just as you were instructed, and overflowing with gratitude.

Colossians 2:6-7 NASB

Sometimes, life here on earth can be complicated, demanding, and busy. When the demands of life leave us rushing from place to place with scarcely a moment to spare, we may fail to pause and say a word of thanks for all the good things we've received. But when we fail to count our blessings, we rob ourselves of the happiness, the peace, and the gratitude that should rightfully be ours.

Today, whether you're on the golf course or any-place else, slow down long enough to start counting your blessings. You most certainly will not be able to count them all, but take a few moments to jot down as many blessings as you can. Then, give thanks to the Giver of all good things: God. His love for you is eternal, as are His gifts. And it's never too soon—or too late—to offer Him thanks.

GREAT IDEAS FROM GOLFING GREATS

Smart golf is winning golf. Cut down on the element of chance.

Walter Hagen

The champion is the fellow who can make the fewest poor shots.

Tommy Armour

It's one thing to be outplayed at golf, and another to be outsmarted.

Doug Sanders

✕ A TIMELY TIP ✕

On the golf course or off, it always pays to be grateful.

─────────────

Therefore, since we receive a kingdom which cannot be shaken, let us show gratitude, by which we may offer to God an acceptable service with reverence and awe....

Hebrews 12:28 NASB

221

THE REWARDS OF WORK

Whatever you do, do it enthusiastically, as something done for the Lord and not for men.

Colossians 3:23 HCSB

Ben Hogan wrote, "There are no born golfers. Some have more natural ability than others, but they've all been made." Hogan, known for his devotion to the practice tee, combined innate ability with relentless preparation. For his efforts, he was rewarded with championship after championship.

The world often promises instant gratification: Get rich—today. Lower your handicap—this week. Have whatever you want—right now. Yet life's experiences and God's Word teach us that the best things in life require heaping helpings of both time and work. It has been said, quite correctly, that there are no shortcuts to any place worth going. So it's important to remember that hard work is not simply a proven way to get ahead, it's also part of God's plan.

Whether it's school, the workplace, or the golf course, preparation is essential. Natural ability is a wonderful thing, but it doesn't guarantee success. In life, as in golf, there's no substitute for hard work.

TODAY'S BIG IDEAS ABOUT GOLF AND LIFE

I cling to a few tattered old virtues, like believing you don't get anything in this world for nothing. This is one of those eternal verities that will be around long after I've sunk my last putt and gone to that great 19th hole in the sky.

Tony Lema

If you want to reach your potential, you need to add a strong work ethic to your talent.

John Maxwell

Think enthusiastically about everything, especially your work.

Norman Vincent Peale

✕ A TIMELY TIP ✕

Wherever you happen to be—whether you're playing golf or actively engaged in the game life—hard work pays off. When you work hard, and keep working hard, you'll earn big rewards.

He did it with all his heart. So he prospered.

2 Chronicles 31:21 NKJV

223

DAY 108

DEFEATING PROCRASTINATION

If you make a promise to God, don't be slow to keep it. God is not happy with fools, so give God what you promised.

Ecclesiastes 5:4 NCV

When tough times arrive, it's easy (and tempting) to avoid those hard-to-do tasks that you would prefer to avoid altogether. If you find yourself bound by the chains of procrastination, ask yourself what you're waiting for—or more accurately what you're afraid of—and why. As you examine the emotional roadblocks that have, heretofore, blocked your path, you may discover that you're waiting for the "perfect" moment, that instant in time when you feel neither afraid nor anxious. But in truth, perfect moments like these are few and far between.

So stop waiting for the perfect moment and focus, instead, on finding the right moment to do what needs to be done. Then, trust God and get busy. When you do, you'll discover that you and the Father, working together, can accomplish great things . . . and that you can accomplish them sooner rather than later.

God has created a world that punishes procrastinators and rewards those who "do it now." In other words, life doesn't procrastinate. Neither should you.

PERFECTING YOUR PUTTING

The man who can putt is a match for anyone.

Willie Park, Jr.

A new putter may work for a few rounds, but eventually the real cause of the problem—technique—comes back to haunt you.

Lee Trevino

Putting allows the touchy golfer two to four opportunities to blow a gasket in the short space of two to forty feet.

Tommy Bolt

✕ A TIMELY TIP ✕

It's easy to put things off, and it's considerably harder to tackle tough jobs. But, unless you learn the importance of doing first things first, you'll never reach your full potential.

If you are too lazy to plow in the right season, you will have no food at the harvest.

Proverbs 20:4 NLT

225

SERVE HIM

The greatest among you will be your servant. Whoever exalts himself will be humbled, and whoever humbles himself will be exalted.

Matthew 23:11-12 HCSB

We live in a world that glorifies power, prestige, fame, and money. But the words of Jesus teach us that the most esteemed men and women in this world are not the self-congratulatory leaders of society but are instead the humblest of servants.

Today, you may feel the temptation to take more than you give. You may be tempted to withhold your generosity. Or you may be tempted to build yourself up in the eyes of your friends. Resist those temptations. Instead, serve your friends quietly and without fanfare. Find a need and fill it . . . humbly. Lend a helping hand . . . anonymously. Share a word of kindness . . . with quiet sincerity. As you go about your daily activities, remember that the Savior of all humanity made Himself a servant, and we, as His followers, must do no less.

Have thy tools ready; God will find thee work.

Charles Kingsley

TODAY'S BIG IDEAS ABOUT GOLF AND LIFE

Nobody asked how you looked, just what you shot.

Sam Snead

If I had it to do over again, I wouldn't beat myself up so much.

Gardner Dickinson

If there's one thing I've learned, it's to play golf your way, instead of playing like somebody else.

Gary Player

TODAY'S SCORE CARD

Jot Down Your Thoughts About . . .
Someone You Can Help Today

_____

_____

_____

_____

_____

_____

_____

NO MORE EXCUSES

If you hide your sins, you will not succeed.

Proverbs 28:13 NCV

We live in a world where excuses are everywhere. And it's precisely because excuses are so numerous that they are also so ineffective. When we hear the words, "I'm sorry but . . . ," most of us know exactly what is to follow: The Big Excuse. The dog ate the homework. Traffic was terrible. It's the company's fault. The boss is to blame. The equipment is broken. We're out of that. And so forth, and so on.

Because we humans are such creative excuse-makers, all of the really good excuses have already been taken. In fact, the high-quality excuses, including the most popular golfing excuses, have been used, re-used, over-used, and abused. That's why excuses don't work—we've heard them all before.

So, if you're wasting your time trying to portray yourself as a victim, or if you're trying to concoct a new and improved excuse, don't bother. Excuses don't work, and while you're inventing them, neither do you.

Replace your excuses with fresh determination.

Charles Swindoll

GREAT IDEAS FROM GOLFING GREATS

Course management is like being in a chess game. You're maneuvering for position.

Patty Sheehan

The secret of low scores is the ability to turn three shots into two.

Bobby Jones

There are no blind holes the second time you play them.

Tommy Armour

✕ A TIMELY TIP ✕

When things don't go well for you, it's tempting to make excuses. Resist that temptation. Just forget the last shot and focus on the next one.

Let us live in a right way . . . clothe yourselves with the Lord Jesus Christ and forget about satisfying your sinful self.

Romans 13:13-14 NCV

THE REWARDS OF DISCIPLINE

Death is the reward of an undisciplined life; your foolish decisions trap you in a dead end.

Proverbs 5:23 MSG

Whether you're playing the game of golf or the game of life, it pays to be disciplined. Self-discipline is not simply a proven way to get ahead; it's also an integral part of God's plan for your life.

If we genuinely seek to be faithful stewards of our time, our talents, and our resources, we must adopt a disciplined approach to life. Otherwise, our talents are wasted and our resources are squandered.

Our greatest rewards result from hard work and perseverance. May we, as disciplined Christians, be willing to work for the rewards we so earnestly desire.

Hoping for a good future without investing in today is like a farmer waiting for a crop without ever planting any seed.

John Maxwell

GREAT IDEAS FROM GOLFING GREATS

Discipline and concentration are a matter of being interested.

Tom Kite

The most important component of good golf is the ability to concentrate.

Dow Finsterwald

Very often, what a man feels he is doing is more important than what he does.

Bobby Jones

TODAY'S SCORE CARD

Jot Down Your Thoughts About . . .
The Rewards of Self-Discipline

PERSPECTIVE FOR TODAY

Don't turn your back on wisdom, for she will protect you. Love her, and she will guard you.

Proverbs 4:6 NLT

Sometimes, amid the demands of daily life, we lose perspective. Life seems out of balance, and the pressures of everyday living seem overwhelming. What's needed is a fresh perspective, a restored sense of balance . . . and God.

If a temporary loss of perspective has left you worried, exhausted, or both, it's time to readjust your thought patterns. Negative thoughts are habit-forming on the golf course or off, but so are positive ones. With practice, you can form the habit of focusing on God's priorities and your possibilities. When you do, you'll soon discover that you will spend less time fretting about your challenges and more time praising God for His gifts.

When you call upon the Lord and prayerfully seek His will, He will give you wisdom and perspective. When you make God's priorities your priorities, He will direct your steps and calm your fears. So today and every day hereafter, pray for a sense of balance and perspective. And remember: your thoughts are intensely powerful things, so handle them with care.

TODAY'S BIG IDEAS ABOUT GOLF AND LIFE

Golf has probably kept more people sane than psychiatrists have.

Harvey Penick

Earthly fears are no fears at all. Answer the big questions of eternity, and the little questions of life fall into perspective.

Max Lucado

For now we see in a mirror, dimly, but then face to face. Now I know in part, but then I shall know just as I also am known.

1 Corinthians 13:12 NKJV

TODAY'S SCORE CARD

Jot Down Your Thoughts About . . .
The Things That Matter Most to You

_____

_____

_____

_____

_____

WORSHIP HIM
EVERY DAY

God is Spirit, and those who worship Him must worship in spirit and truth.

John 4:24 HCSB

God's Word makes it clear: we should offer our Creator the praise and worship He deserves—and we shouldn't wait until Sunday morning to do so. Yet we live in a distraction-filled society that encourages us to make praise and worship a one-day-a-week activity.

Do you take time each day to worship your Father in heaven, or do you wait until Sunday morning to praise Him for His blessings? The answer to this question will, in large part, determine the quality and direction of your spiritual life in good times and in turbulent times.

Every day provides opportunities to put God where He belongs: at the center of our lives. When we do so, we worship Him not only with our words, but also with our deeds, and that's as it should be. For believers, God comes first. Always first.

Worship is a daunting task. Each worships differently. But each should worship.

Max Lucado

GREAT IDEAS FROM GOLFING GREATS

When you're playing poorly, you start thinking too much. That's when you confuse yourself.

Greg Norman

When in trouble, play the shot you know you can play, not the shot you hope you can play.

Jack Burke, Jr.

Every golfer can expect to have four bad shots a round. When you do, just put them out of your mind.

Walter Hagen

TODAY'S SCORE CARD

Jot Down Your Thoughts About . . .
The Rewards of Worship

_____

_____

_____

_____

_____

_____

THE POWER OF A POSITIVE EXAMPLE

Set an example of good works yourself, with integrity and dignity in your teaching.

Titus 2:7 HCSB

Whether we like it or not, all of us are role models. What kind of example are you? Are you a person whose behavior serves as a positive role model for others? Are you the kind of person whose actions, on the golf course or off, are based upon kindness, faithfulness, and the Golden Rule? If so, you are not only blessed by God, but you are also a powerful force for good in a world that desperately needs positive influences such as yours.

Corrie ten Boom advised, "Don't worry about what you do not understand. Worry about what you do understand in the Bible but do not live by." And that's sound advice because our families and friends are watching . . . and so, for that matter, is God.

Let us preach you, Dear Jesus, without preaching, not by words but by our example, by the casting force, the sympathetic influence of what we do.

Mother Teresa

GREAT IDEAS FROM GOLFING GREATS

Golf is like solitaire. When you cheat, you only cheat yourself.

Tony Lema

Eighteen holes of match or medal play will teach you more about your foe than will 18 years of dealing with him across a desk.

Grantland Rice

Golf tells you much about character. Play a round of golf with someone, and you know them more intimately than you might from years of dinner parties.

Harvey Penick

✕ A TIMELY TIP ✕

Whether you're playing a round of golf, or doing just about anything else for that matter, other people are watching. So be the kind of example that God wants you to be: a good example.

_____

You should be an example to the believers in speech, in conduct, in love, in faith, in purity.

1 Timothy 4:12 HCSB

FOLLOW HIM

Then Jesus said to His disciples, "If anyone wants to come with Me, he must deny himself, take up his cross, and follow Me. For whoever wants to save his life will lose it, but whoever loses his life because of Me will find it."

Matthew 16:24-25 HCSB

Jesus walks with you. Are you walking with Him seven days a week, and not just on Sunday mornings? Are you a seven-day-a-week Christian who carries your faith with you to work each day, or do you try to keep Jesus at a "safe" distance when you're not sitting in church? Hopefully, you understand the wisdom of walking with Christ all day every day.

Jesus loved you so much that He endured unspeakable humiliation and suffering for you. How will you respond to Christ's sacrifice? Will you take up His cross and follow Him—during good times and tough times—or will you choose another path? When you place your hopes squarely at the foot of the cross, when you place Jesus squarely at the center of your life, you will be blessed.

Do you seek to fulfill God's purpose for your life? Do you seek spiritual abundance? Would you like to partake in "the peace that passes all understanding"? Then follow Christ. Follow Him by picking up His cross today and every day that you live. When you do, you will quickly discover that Christ's love has the power to change everything, including you.

TODAY'S BIG IDEAS ABOUT GOLF AND LIFE

For when the one Great Scorer comes to write against your name, He marks not that you won or lost, but how you played the game.

Grantland Rice

You who suffer take heart. Christ is the answer to sorrow.

Billy Graham

 A TIMELY TIP

Think about your relationship with Jesus: what it is, and what it can be. Then, as you embark upon the next phase of your life's journey, be sure to walk with your Savior every step of the way.

Then he told them what they could expect for themselves: "Anyone who intends to come with me has to let me lead."

Luke 9:23 MSG